Mindscape

EXPLORING THE REALITY OF
THOUGHT FORMS

Mindscape

Bruce A. Vance

*This publication made possible with
the assistance of the Kern Foundation*

The Theosophical Publishing House
Wheaton, Ill. U.S.A.
Madras, India/London, England

Library of Congress Cataloging in Publication Data

Vance, Bruce A., 1953-
    Mindscape : exploring the reality of thought forms / Bruce A.
Vance. – 1st ed.
        p.   cm. – (Quest books)
    Includes bibliographical references.
    ISBN 0-8356-0660-0 (pbk.) : $9.95
    1. Mind and body. 2. Reality.   3. Symbolism (Psychology)
4. Thought and thinking.   I. Title.
BF161.V35   1990
133.8 – dc20   90-50201
                                                          CIP

Printed in the United States of America

To Sharon

Contents

Preface

The most mysterious aspect of human existence is the mind. An understanding of its nature is of utmost importance, since the mind is the key to, and instrument for, all our relationships with reality. Still, it remains a relatively unexplored enigma. Psychologists and psychiatrists attempt to delve into its mysteries by examining the behavior, thoughts, and emotions of individuals. But such an approach is necessarily indirect—it addresses only the mind's apparent effects. Is there, perhaps, a way in which we can study the nature of the mind directly?

No one can see into another's mind. Therefore, any direct approach to the study of mind must be undertaken by each individual. We all have direct access to our own minds; we alone can penetrate the mysteries of our own thoughts, feelings, beliefs, and attitudes. We may be able to make use of the theories and discoveries of others in our personal psychology, applying techniques and comparing our mental machinations with those of others. But in the last analysis only you hold the keys to your own mind, and only you can unlock every door.

There is a critical issue facing any investigator of

the mind and its nature: how real are the contents of the mind? We know we have thoughts, feelings, and beliefs, but do we know their natures? Do we know how real they are? Some scientists would have us view our thoughts as electrical charges resulting from chemical interactions. Others altogether avoid the issue by saying that the machinations of the mind are subjective phenomena which have no essential reality: if no one else can see or perceive your thoughts, then your thoughts must be unreal. But do either of these approaches really solve the riddles that confront us?

You know that your thoughts and emotions are real, although you may not know in what way they are real. The activities of your mind have a profound effect on every aspect of your life. What you think and feel determines how you perceive the world and yourself. Your daydreams and fantasies can bring you happiness; your pessimism and fears can bring you depression. Your emotions and thoughts affect your body. No one can dispute the fact that the contents of your mind have a real effect upon who you are and how you relate to reality.

The effects of thoughts and emotions go even farther than this. Have you noticed their infectious nature? When we are around someone who is optimistic, cheerful, and inspired, we feel better, unless our own mood at the time is so overwhelmingly dark that we are closed off to outside, positive influences. And when we are in the proximity of someone who is depressed or pessimistic, we feel our own thoughts and feelings grow darker. It seems that the contents of an individual's mind have a direct effect upon the contents of another's mind.

Anything that affects other things must have a reality beyond the subjective or hallucinatory. It must have an objective reality, and it must have observable properties and characteristics. Its actions and effects must be governed by some discernible laws, so that it somehow fits into the continuum that is the infinite order of all that is.

That thoughts, emotions, and the other aspects of mind have an objective reality and viable effects in the world at large is not a new concept. A belief in the objective reality of thoughts and emotions has existed throughout recorded history. The clairvoyant Charles W. Leadbeater said: "Everybody, when it occurs to him, recognizes the indirect action of thought, for it is obvious that a man must think before he can do anything, and the thought is the motive power of his act just as the water is the motive power of the mill. But people do not generally know that thought has also a direct action on matter—that whether or not a man translates his thought into a deed, the thought itself has already produced an effect."[1]

Buddhist doctrine goes so far as to proclaim that all is mind. According to Christmas Humphreys: "Man, as the greatest minds have ever perceived, is a microcosm of the universal Macrocosm—'As above so below'—and cosmic psychology, if one may so describe it, is the foundation of human psychology. In the Mahayana the doctrine of Mind-Only figures largely. All is Mind, and the stuff of the world is mind-stuff. It follows that 'all that we are is the result of what we have thought.' But not only are we the product of our thinking, but the world around us has no validity for us save as the product of that Mind of which each 'mind' is a partial manifestation."[2] This same concept is echoed in the words of Ralph Waldo Emerson: "Nature is the incarnation of a thought, and turns to a thought, again, as ice becomes water and gas. The world is mind precipitated, and the volatile essence is forever escaping again into the state of free thought."[3]

More recently Carl Jung hypothesized the existence of a psychic energy—which, however, he conceived of as being physically based—and said that he was "in entire agreement with von Grot—one of the first to propose the concept of psychic energy—when he says: 'The concept of psychic energy is as much justified in science as that of physical energy, and psychic energy has just as many quantitative measurements and different forms as has physical energy.' "[4] In the same article, while discussing the possibility of an energetic component to psychic activities, he added: "The almost universal incidence of the primitive concept of energy is a clear expression of the fact that even at early levels of human consciousness man felt the need to represent the sensed dynamism of psychic events in a concrete way. If, therefore, in our psychology we lay stress on the energetic point of view, this is in accord with the psychic facts which have been graven on the mind of man since primordial times."[5]

Perhaps you think it does not matter whether thoughts are real. What practical bearing could it have on your life? A few considerations suggest an answer to this question.

Could it be that each thought you hold in your mind has the power to attract similar thoughts and to repel dissimilar thoughts? Could your desires serve as energetic magnets, drawing events into your life? Could it be that your overall belief system operates like a web of energy within the mind, having a predetermined effect on everything you experience? Could this web limit what you are able to perceive by filtering out everything not compatible with itself? And aside from the effects the energy of your thoughts and emotions have upon yourself, what effects does it have on others as a result of the energies you transmit with your mind?

If thoughts and the other creations of mind and consciousness have an objective reality, then the practical implications are endless. To what degree do we create our own reality? Can we more effectively organize our lives through an understanding and use of the powers of mind? What responsibilities do we have in regard to the thoughts and emotions we transmit to the world? How do our own beliefs limit us in our perceptions of reality? Obviously, if our thoughts are more than subjective phantoms, we have much to consider.

Part I

1

Basic Contents of Mind

The nature of mind has been investigated since at least the beginning of recorded history, and probably since reflection became a part of human experience. We can understand nothing unless it is by way of the mind; all our perceptions must be assimilated within the mind. Philosophers have always grappled with the issues of perception, knowledge, and thinking, though they have reached little consensus. As Descartes said, "[philosophy] has been cultivated for many centuries by the best minds that have ever lived, . . . nevertheless no single thing is to be found in it that is not subject of dispute."[1]

If the philosophers have failed to come to a clear understanding of the nature of mind, how can we presume to tackle the problem? I believe we have little choice in the matter. If we are ever to understand ourselves, we must investigate the nature of our own minds. We need not expect to find all the answers. The corridors of mind are endless, and an exploration of them must be a task equally endless. However, as the saying goes, each journey must begin with a single step.

Our first step, then, must involve taking a look at

those aspects of the mind which are familiar and easily engaged. We know that the mind is filled with thoughts, emotions, attitudes, and beliefs. We can observe these by simply turning our attention inward; they are immediate and easily accessible. But do we really know what they are? We give expression to our thoughts in words or images. And we express our attitudes and opinions with words and pictures. We give names to our emotions. But in doing these things we are expressing the contents of the mind in physical terms. What is the nature of a thought before it is expressed?

We can think without ever verbalizing our thoughts, and we can have opinions that we never put into words. It would seem, then, that the contents of the mind have an objective reality before they are given form, that our thoughts and our other mental constructs have an existence prior to their physical expression. They are not unreal; they are not phantoms. Obviously their existence is not physical; nevertheless they are more than subjective inner hallucinations. They have an objectively valid existence which may be observed, studied, and hopefully, understood.

OBJECTIVE REALITY OF THE CONTENTS OF MIND

Where might we find evidence to support the concept of the objective reality of thoughts and other mental constructs? Some of the most striking evidence comes to us by way of the research done with telepathy, or thought-transference, and psychokinesis, or the effect of mind upon matter. Although telepathy has yet to be accepted as a fact by the scientific community, research indicates that it is a demonstrable phenomenon.

In the 1930s J. B. Rhine of Duke University led one of the first teams in the research of telepathy. Their investigations involved numerous experiments under controlled conditions and yielded the most thorough documentation of the phenomenon of extrasensory perception (ESP) that had been seen up to that time. The results of the research done by Rhine and his associates was startling; it challenged the long-held assumption that all knowledge must be obtained through the physical senses. Rhine said: "The research represents a critical testing of this dogma of the inviolability of the mind's sensory frontier. If we could find any extra-sensory avenue to knowledge, not only would that concept cease to be the circumscribing law of mind it was once considered, but a new frontier, a further horizon would be established."

"That new frontier has now been established unless all of us who have been exploring it by years of testing and many hundreds of thousands of trials have been completely and continuingly self-deluded or incompetent, not only at the Duke laboratory but elsewhere as well. Either delusion is the explanation of our results or else we have found proof that the mind of man does indeed have an extra-sensory way of perceiving, and hence, whether we like it or not, the old frontier must go the way of Newtonian mechanics in the light of relativity."[2]

The research at Duke University expanded to include such phenomena as clairvoyance and psychokinesis. Louisa E. Rhine, J. B. Rhine's wife and co-worker at Duke, published a book in 1970 detailing the continuing research in the field of psychokinesis. In this work she says: "The evidence is in. The case for PK [psychokinesis] has been presented, at least in outline. In experiment after experiment statistically significant scores were obtained. The objects used in the tests would not have behaved the way they did by chance alone. Unexpected as the verdict may be, the only reasonable explanation for the results of the tests was that they were affected by the will of the subjects."[3]

Many people have experienced occasional evidence of telepathy in their own lives. Individuals who have lived together for a long period of time commonly experience shared thinking. Parents have reported being aware of their children's illnesses before being informed of the fact. Simple experiences like knowing that someone is going to call you before the phone rings also demonstrate the existence of telepathy.

So, if telepathy and psychokinesis are real we are led to the conclusion that thoughts must have some sort of energetic property which allows for their transmission and reception. A mother sensing that her child is in danger implies that emotions or feelings must also have a transmissible energetic quality. Clearly, if one accepts extrasensory perception as a reality, then one must also accept the objective reality of mental creations.

Some aspects of dreaming also support this thesis. In one section of *Dreamscape: Voyage in an Alternate Reality*[4] I discuss shared dreams, a phenomenon wherein one dreamer may perceive the self-created dream images of another dreamer. If our mentally created dream images can be perceived by others, does this not also point to the objective reality of mental creations? The bulk of our self-created dreams involve us in perceiving our thoughts and feelings as they are projected in a nonphysical dimension. At such times we are obtaining clear subjective evidence of the very real nature of our mental creations.

The same holds true for prayer. What are your prayers but mentally generated thoughts and feelings? If you believe that you can send messages to God or to saints, then you must already believe in the objective reality of thoughts and feelings. You must also hold the belief that thoughts may be transmitted from one mind to another, and thus you believe in telepathy, whether or not you recognize it as such.

But perhaps the strongest evidence in support of the concept that thoughts, ideas, and feelings have an objective reality lies in the reasonableness of the concept. Until we have more solid proof in this area, perhaps we should trust to our own sense of what is true and reasonable. Is it reasonable to assume that thoughts floating around in your mind are mere hallucinations with no power, no reality? Or is it more reasonable to believe that they have a kind of reality of their own, some energetic power which makes it possible for them to affect you and others?

If you cannot at present fully believe in the objective reality of your mental creations, I hope that by the time you finish reading this book you will be able to. Perhaps you will find concepts that help explain things that previously made no sense to you, and as a result you may come to accept the reality of thoughts. If you already believe in the objective reality of your mental creations, then I hope this material will serve to increase your understanding of your own creations.

BASIC CHARACTERISTICS OF THOUGHT-FORMS

If thoughts do indeed have an objective reality, what is their nature? We know from science that in the final analysis our world is composed of energy. However solid things may appear, they consist of packets of energy, or quanta. It is reasonable to assume, therefore, that thoughts also must consist of some type of energy. Labeling this energy will not make it understandable, of course, but it will make it easier to talk about. Thoughts are products of the mind, so we may safely say that they are composed of mental energy.

In any discussion of the nature of mental energy,

we are handicapped by having to use words that are associated traditionally with physical rather than mental phenomena. In an attempt to prevent unnecessary confusion, I want to define and clarify a few of the terms in this book.

Thought-form. A discrete bundle of mental energy of relatively limited scope and content, generally containing only one item of information.

Mental construct or **mental construction.** Any mental creation, such as a thought-form, idea, belief, or other complex mental creation, composed of mental energy.

Mental energy field. A field analogous to an energy field in physics, in which lines of electrical or magnetic force are active. In the case of mental energy, the lines are composed of forces of attraction and repulsion plus connective streams of mental or psychic energy. These interact according to field dynamics.

Lines of power or **lines of force.** Interconnective mental energies that link various thought-forms and mental constructs or provide paths of interaction.

Operational system or **operational pattern.** An individual's complex mental construction that guides his or her behavior. Includes one's fundamental beliefs and conceptions regarding reality.

These terms and concepts will become clearer in the course of this book. For now, let's return to the simplest unit of mental energy—the thought-form.

Most thoughts, as you probably know, are not isolated units. Instead, you produce a nearly continuous stream of mental energy with a wide variety of pulsations and fluctuations. The term "stream of consciousness" hints at the nature of this flow of energy. Your thoughts often wind about from one subject to another as various associations occur to you. Or as you think about something, for no apparent reason you find yourself thinking about something entirely different which has no identifiable association with the previous thought.

Because of the fluidity of the mental processes and the way our thoughts are generated in a continuous stream, it is somewhat misleading to look at the nature of an isolated thought-form, but we need to approach thoughts in this way so that the complexities of the mental processes do not overwhelm us before we understand the basics. After exploring the characteristics of isolated thought-forms, I will discuss the ways in which thoughts intermingle and form the streams of consciousness with which you are familiar.

The "Shape" of Thoughts

A thought does not have a single, unvarying form as a physical object does. Consider telepathy: in mind-to-mind communication information is rarely transmitted or received as concrete images or words. Instead, the tone and intention are transmitted; the information is relayed as a "bundle" that carries the basic meaning. The recipient is left to translate that information into terms to which he or she may relate. We might imagine such a thought-form as shaped like a cloud. When this "thought-cloud" is received or translated by an individual, it is given more specific shape or form in accordance with that individual's mental and psychic make-up.

Joseph Chilton Pearce, in *Exploring the Crack in the Cosmic Egg*,[5] discusses an experiment in telepathy he performed with about a half-dozen people. In one instance he was looking at a drawing of a circle with a square cross in it, and he asked the others to describe what he saw. One individual saw a wagon wheel with incomplete spokes, a musician-artist saw a flower blossom from the stem side, and one woman saw a circle with the cross under it. In other experiments the same phenomenon was encountered: each individual picked up the basic image but translated it into a form unique to his or her own mental make-up.

Various factors affect the relative clarity or intensity of specific thought-forms or thought-clouds, and I will discuss these later. For now you need to recognize that thoughts are fields of energy which only take on generally recognizable "shapes" when they are "read" or entertained within the mind of an individual. There are, of course, some very specific and narrow cases in which a thought may be said to have a definite, unaltering shape, as when one thinks of an equilateral triangle. But even in this case the thought itself allows for a wide variety of characteristics, such as size and color.

You will not directly experience the cloudlike shape of thoughts unless you are able to perceive nonphysical dimensions. Clairvoyants such as Annie Besant and Charles Leadbeater have written detailed descriptions of thought-forms they could perceive, and the practicing clairvoyant would do well to investigate their research and that of other clairvoyants. You will encounter mostly thoughts within your own mind that have been automatically translated into a shape or placed within a context that you can recognize. But it is important to bear in mind that thoughts are fields of energy, since this will directly relate to some of the characteristics of thoughts and other creations of mind and consciousness.

Information Content

One of the most obvious aspects of any particular field of mental energy is the information that is carried or conveyed by it. Such information may be stored in the form of a memory, an image, a concept, or an idea; but whatever its form, it exists primarily as mental energy. In many cases this information is translated by us into words, since we are a language-oriented people. At other times it may take on the characteristics of a simple mental picture or image, as when the information involves the image of another person's face. These, however, are the ways we perceive the information as it is translated in terms relating to our experiences in physical reality.

The information composing a mental construction may be simple or complex. The more complex the information, however, the more likely is it that we are dealing with a combination of mental energy fields or a gestalt, rather than with an isolated thought-form. But the principle of information conveyance remains the same in either case.

Some mental forms contain information which is of a purely intellectual nature, appearing dry or lifeless due to the lack of any significant emotional energy. For example, the thought-form conveying "four plus four equals eight" is a simple mental construction with very little emotional power in and of itself. On the other hand, there are other thoughts which carry an almost inherent subjective, emotional punch. The thought of death immediately gives rise to a multitude of feelings and therefore may be said to have high levels of incipient energy.

The information contained within any thought-form or thought-gestalt determines the configuration of energy or patterns of energy within the field. Once again employing the image of a cloud—the swirls, flows and interminglings of currents within that cloud are determined by the patterns of information. These configurations are instantaneously generated by and held in the mind on the production or reception of a thought.

Emotional Coloring

Each cluster of mental energy, then, carries information, and this information gives rise to emotional energy. Rarely do we think about anything without having some feeling about that subject. The feelings that arise in association with each thought serve to color it—to imbue it with a frequency of vibration which may be perceived in a number of different ways.

If you could see a thought-form or a mental construct as it exists within the nonphysical dimensions, you would perceive a variety of colors within it. According to Leadbeater: "Elemental essence when molded by thought adopts a certain color—a color which is expressive of the nature of the thought or feeling."[6] These colors correspond to the emotional and feeling vibrations with which the thought is imbued, just as physical objects have colors that correspond to the frequency of the light which they reflect.

Perceiving the emotional character of a mental construction involves resonating frequencies. When you receive or entertain a thought-form, a portion of your consciousness resonates at the same frequency as the thought-form, thus permitting you to feel its nature. Also, when you generate a mental energy field you simultaneously cause it to vibrate in accordance with the feelings you have about it.

For example, in Emerson's essays there are strong emotional tones pervading the words he has written.

The words themselves are simple carriers of information, but that information is imbued with the powerful energies of the writer, and it is structured in such a way as to naturally arouse strong emotions. As you read such works your own emotions are stirred as you resonate to the feelings interwoven with the message. In the same way, all mental constructions carry a tone and color corresponding to the emotion with which they are imbued.

The colors of thought-forms and their complementary emotions, like their shapes, can be directly perceived only by a clairvoyant, a nonphysical traveller, or an individual with well-developed intuitive faculties. Generally these colors are translated into the feelings with which we are all familiar. However, we tend to associate colors with emotions—green with envy, yellow with cowardice, red with anger, a brown study, or a black mood. Of course, these are simplified versions of the complexities of color inherent in mental energy fields, but they do provide evidence of our intuitive recognition of the nonphysical coloring provided by emotional energies.

Intensity

Another aspect of mental creations is their relative intensity. Thought-forms take on greater intensity through a variety of methods. One of these methods involves emotional charging.

If you feel strongly about something, you fill the thought of that thing or event with an abundance of energy. For example, for each of us there are particular moments in our lives which we will always remember with clarity and intensity—your first kiss, or a favorite childhood pet. These events are associated with strong emotions. Because you felt strongly about these things, their memory is stored in your mind with greater energy, and thus they remain with you for a long time. So, strong emotion can increase the intensity of a thought-form or mental construct.

Repetition also increases the intensity of energy in a mental field. At one time or another we have all had to memorize something. We repeated it mentally over and over until it was strong enough to remain with us. The simple act of repeatedly thinking of a thing increases its intensity. Anyone who has used the technique of repeating a mantra will recognize this process.

One-pointedness will also intensify a mental energy field. This is similar to the process of repetition, but instead of repeating the thought, you make a shortcut by excluding all distracting thoughts and for a short period focus the full force of your mental powers upon the chosen thought-form. Usually our minds wander or are distracted, and we have to use repetition to enforce a thought. By focusing the mind on one point for just a short period of time we accomplish the same increase in intensity as we would through a long period of repetition.

The relative intensity of a mental energy field determines its staying power and its degree of influence within your mind. The intensity of thoughts directed toward the achievement of some goal plays a strong part in determining the thought's effectiveness. I will discuss this in more detail later. Finally, in terms of telepathy, the intensity of thought-forms plays a key part in others being able to pick up thoughts directed for this purpose.

Clarity

As we all know, some people can express an idea more clearly than others. In the same way mental formulations and isolated thought-forms have different degrees of clarity. Logical coherence manifests one type of clarity; well-defined mental imagery brings about another type. The degree to which we understand a concept also determines how clearly we are able to hold that concept within the mind.

A lack of clarity and cohesion within a mental energy field will tend to make it dissipate more quickly. Doubt and points of confusion may allow tangential thoughts to impinge upon it, pulling it apart. One might say that the structural integrity of a thought-form is determined by its clarity and inner cohesion. When a thought or mental energy field is clear, precise, and self-consistent, it has a greater structural integrity and is more likely to hold its form, as well as to convey its meaning and contents.

Each of the characteristics of a mental energy field affects all of the others. A clearly defined thought is easier to concentrate upon and therefore can be more easily increased in power and intensity. Likewise, we can't very well imbue a thought-form with emotional energy if it is so lacking in clarity that we're not sure what we are thinking about. Obviously, a mental structure can more effectively carry information if that information is clear in the mind of the one who generates it.

The degree of clarity and cohesion in the energy field determines the clarity of a thought-form: the energy currents, charges, and fluctuations are more or less clearly defined. Also, the boundaries of the energy field composing a particular thought-form will be more clearly defined if the overall idea is clearly conceived. A mental energy field lacking clarity and precision will more easily bleed off into associated or tangential energy fields than will one with greater clarity.

Finally, there are other less obvious characteristics

of any mental energy field, some of which I will discuss later. There are polarities, charges, and fluctuations of a nearly infinite variety, and these serve not only to stimulate us mentally in myriad ways, but also to determine how a mental energy field will behave in the presence of other thought-forms and mental constructs. As mentioned earlier, thoughts give rise to associated thoughts and feelings. In order to understand these patterns of association, as well as some of the more complex energy states within isolated mental energy fields, we have to look at the ways in which thought-forms interact and intermingle.

THE INTERACTIVE PROPERTIES OF MENTAL ENERGY FIELDS

Mental energy fields, like everything else, do not stand alone, but exist in relation to many other things. They affect and are affected by the mind that generates or entertains them. And they naturally interact in a variety of ways with other mental energy fields. Also, and this is discussed in Chapter 7, they influence the very reality systems in which we exist.

The thoughts that occur to us and that we hold within our minds do not arise out of nothingness. As explained, the mental realm, like the physical, is composed of energy. Leadbeater names this nonphysical energy "elemental essence."[7] For simplicity I call it "mental energy." We impress or organize it according to our experiences, both physical and nonphysical, which provide us with the material—the events, ideas, concepts, impressions—which we use to compose the ongoing stream of mental constructions.

Each experience, then, impresses mental energy. As we think and communicate with others, we often use language—a man-made set of symbols—for the purpose of representing our experiences. Also, in the course of our lives we perceive a multitude of images, some of which are imprinted within the mind and carried with us throughout life. All of these experiences, the impressions they leave, and the language-symbols representing them become the building blocks of our overall mental matrix.

When we formulate an idea we arrange component parts of our experiential impressions into new gestalts of mental energy. We are forever correlating and assimilating our experiential impressions and rearranging them in new ways, in order to find new and greater perspectives on existence. The simplest thought of "two plus two equals four" rises out of a vast field of experience which includes our total understanding of mathematics and our recognition and employment of agreed-upon symbols. And even the thought of a box requires that we draw upon the experiences encountered through our physical senses, and our understanding of three-dimensional reality.

An isolated thought-form is created when we direct innumerable channels of mental energy to one area, where they combine and form a relatively self-contained energy field, which we may then call a thought, a desire, or an idea. This new thought-form becomes a new fluctuation or current within our total mental field. Having currents, polarities, and energy charges, it begins to affect other regions of the mind.

Attraction and Repulsion

A mental energy field may draw new component parts to itself, increasing its scope and range, and thus giving rise to new ideas within the mind. Let's say that you were the first to realize the existence of the law of gravity, that you discovered that physical objects had a pull upon each other. From this realization you might go on to realize that this force of gravity shows itself in a multitude of ways, from the planets in their orbits to the falling of raindrops. Thus, the original mental formulation gave rise to innumerable other thoughts related to and derived from the original.

Thought-forms attract similar or associated thought-forms. As Leadbeater says, "Thoughts on the same subject and of the same character tend to aggregate."[8] If you think of one beautiful thing it will give rise to thoughts of other beautiful things. If you entertain the emotion of love, you will likely begin to think of all the times you have been in love. Thus one mental energy field can draw or attract an endless chain of similar or related energy fields. Because of this subtle magnetic force, thought-forms naturally grow and give rise to new realizations and associations. This force also has more far-reaching effects, as I discuss later.

The energy field which composes a mental construc-tion also has repelling or exclusive properties. For the present, this force can best be seen by looking at a more complicated grouping of mental energy fields. Consider your overall belief system as an intercon-nected network of thought-forms—a subject I discuss in more detail later. This belief network, then, will exclude all concepts and ideas from your mind which do not fit into it. The gridwork of your resident belief system will repel beliefs and ideas that are contrary to the beliefs you maintain.

Perhaps a simpler way of seeing this repelling force is to consider your state of mind when you are de-pressed or in a pessimistic frame of mind. So long as you entertain and focus your attention on negative thought-forms or negative mental energy fields, posi-tive thoughts will be unable to surface or appear within your mind. Negative mental energies can literally repel positive thoughts, while at the same time they draw other negative thoughts into your mind. Thus, mental energy fields not only attract similar mental energies, they also repel dissimilar ones.

Interconnections through Association

Another way in which mental energy fields connect and interact is by way of association. Let's say that you are thinking of a rose. Subsequently there may arise in your mind the thought of a particularly lovely rose garden which you once saw. You may then think of a bouquet of roses which you once gave or received. It should be easy to see in such a case how associations have given rise to new thoughts.

As explained, within the structure of a thought-form, or of any mental energy field, there are a number of energy currents and vibrations. The particular mental energy swirl which constitutes the thought of a rose will elicit other thoughts, memories, or impressions which also have that particular energy pattern as part of their make-up. Various thought-forms, therefore, may connect or be connected only partially, but enough so that the thought of the one thing will elicit the thought of the other.

These connections through association are part of the reason why telepathic communications may seem to be distorted. If, for example, either consciously or unconsciously, you pick up someone else's thought-form, you may alter it in your mind as a result of divergent associations. Though you attune yourself to a particular portion of that thought-form, it may evoke an associated event from your own life. Another person's thought of a rose, for example, may give rise in your mind to your receiving or giving a rose. Connections through association may occur between thought-forms during the process of telepathic communication.

Connections between mental energy fields may arise

in a variety of ways. They may be due solely to the associations which you make between different mental images, feelings, or thoughts as a result of your own experiences and attitudes. Or they may result from an inherent relationship between different types of thought-forms, as when the thought of a square gives rise to the thought of a cube. And finally, associations may occur obliquely, as when the thought of a rose makes you think of someone you know who is named Rose.

However the associations arise, they produce interconnections between mental energy fields within your mind and create a virtual webwork of energy lines and flows. Because of these connections, conscious, directed thinking requires concentration so that the attention will not be sidetracked along these various channels or lines of force. At times one may choose to follow these lines of association, letting the mind wander down one path of association after another, in order to detect and understand the patterns that exist within one's mind.

Ultimately everything is related to everything else. Therefore, all mental energy fields are interconnected, either directly or indirectly, by channels of association. Conceivably, you could explore all the corridors of your mind simply by exploring associations, no matter where you started. Such a process, however, would involve taking the long road of discovery. Fortunately, our mental energies are organized in ways that make mental explorations easier and more direct.

MENTAL GESTALTS AND STREAMS OF THOUGHT

Thus far I have discussed the nature of thoughts and mental energy fields in a necessarily simplistic manner. As mentioned before, it is rare to entertain an isolated thought or emotion. Our mental framework is far too complex and our thoughts and feelings are far too interwoven to allow us full understanding by examining thought-forms in a piecemeal manner only. But this approach has been necessary in order to present a basic conception of the nature of mental energy fields, and of the ways in which they interact and interrelate.

If you consider the concept of an isolated energy field composing a thought-form, it should be easy to extend this picture and visualize a grouping of energy fields into what can be termed a "mental gestalt of energy." A gestalt is an integration or grouping of parts into an organic or relatively cohesive whole.

We generally arrange the mental energy of our thoughts and feelings into such gestalts. When, for example, you think about your family, you immediately elicit a wide variety of thoughts and emotions. You may think of your past experiences with members of your family. You may also think of the present and possible future experiences and relationships with them. There may be sadness mixed with joy, mixed with hope and expectations. With the thought of family you have brought into play a large gestalt of mental energies that make up your total field of experiences in relation to your family.

Again, when you think of such a simple thing as a box, you unconsciously invoke quite a number of mental energy fields. The very word "box" requires that you draw upon your understanding of each of the letters in the word—the sounds of each letter and the fact that this word represents a tangible object. And you have to draw upon your experiences of having seen boxes so that you can visualize one in your mind. This implies understanding three-dimensional reality.

So our thoughts and other mental constructions are

actually groupings of smaller energy fields into larger ones. The issues of attractions, repulsions and associations immediately become more complex. Each gestalt of mental energy has a large number of points at which associated thoughts and feelings may connect, or from which new associations may be derived. The currents, fluctuationś, and intensities of energy within these more complex fields likewise become more complex. Fields within fields mix and interact until a new and relatively stable field of greater dimensions is established. Only then do you actually have what we commonly think of as a thought or a feeling.

Now, just as thought-forms do not stand alone, mental gestalts do not stand alone, even after they have become a stable package of information and power. There are always lines of mental energy connecting every mental gestalt with innumerable others. Each thought or idea or feeling you entertain is connected to all of the experiences that have served to bring about that thought or feeling.

Though this is becoming complicated, we still must go further in order to begin to understand the dynamics of mind. When we think, we generally do so sequentially. One thought and its associated feelings is quickly followed by another thought and its associated feelings. We string our thoughts together like beads on a chain in a virtually unending stream.

These streams of mental energy which compose our lines of thinking and feeling have their own field dynamics. New tributaries may enter into the main stream at any time. The stream may wind along a convoluted course, or it may flow in a direct, straightforward channel, as when you are concentrating on a particular issue or idea, enforcing discipline on the flow of your thoughts. Commonly, however, we let our stream of thinking be directed by the whims of association. While we are thinking about one thing, something associated occurs to us, and the mental stream goes off in a new direction. At other times there may be spontaneous breaks in the flow of our mental streams. Some external stimulus may lead us to forget what we were thinking about, thus breaking the flow of our thoughts and starting a new stream of mental energy. All these streams, then, are what we call the flow of our thoughts.

Like thought-forms and mental gestalts, mental streams have complex field dynamics. Points of association are numerous. Potentials for mental attraction and repulsion increase nearly exponentially. And the currents and fluctuations are so varied and complex that the possibilities for divergent streams of thought and feeling seem numberless. It is no wonder that it takes a good deal of mental effort in order to concentrate and to keep our line of thinking along a desired channel.

Now, so far I have discussed primarily only those mental energy fields we generate or entertain from moment to moment. Obviously, we have a vast storehouse of thoughts, emotions, attitudes, and beliefs we do not consciously entertain or use each moment. Where are these located, and how do they figure into our day-to-day lives? How do the simple characteristics of thought-forms relate to our wide-ranging belief systems? What are the overall structures of our mental matrices, and how do they affect our perception of reality?

I hope to answer these questions in the ensuing chapters. To that end I now step back from the complexity of the field dynamics of mental energy and investigate the nature of mind itself.

2

The Domain of Mind

We speak of having something "in mind" or "on our minds," but where and what is this thing we call mind? It seems to be in the head, but this is because the brain is the connecting organ between the mind and body. However, many leading thinkers agree now that the mind is not physical and cannot really be part of the brain.* It must instead exist in a dimension beyond the reach of the physical senses, just as the thoughts and emotions do.

At first it may seem difficult to conceive of a dimension of reality beyond the physical since we are so involved and focused within the material dimension. But our thoughts, emotions, and even our dreams give us a glimpse of the ephemeral realm of mind. We speak of going on flights of fancy, and in doing so we reveal a natural recognition of the possibility that the mind and its locale are of such a nature as to permit inner journeys. And we are all familiar with the process of going inward, of going "into" the mind.

By simply turning our attention inward, we can get a fair feeling for the spaciousness of the mind's realm.

*See for example, J. C. Eccles and D. N. Robinson, *The Wonder of Being Human* (Boston: Shambhala, 1984).

Boundaries in this mysterious place seem nonexistent. However, we can perceive landmarks, or their equivalent: we have memories which we can locate again and again. Experiences seem to reside in specific regions, faithfully awaiting our efforts at recall. And beliefs seem to be stored deeply, where they quietly dictate our actions.

So we already have a sense of the mind's inner reaches. We may not know exactly where the mindscape exists in relation to our position in physical reality, but we know that the door into it always remains open and that we may enter its depths at any time. Perhaps if we go through that doorway we can get a better idea of what lies beyond.

MENTAL SPACE AND THE WEBWORK OF THE PERSONAL MIND-MATRIX

Close your eyes and try to find some memory which you have not thought about for a long time, perhaps of your first day at school or of your first pet. You will find yourself involved in a search, just as if you were flipping through the pages of a book in an attempt to find a particular passage. Your conscious attention searches through the corridors of your mind, passing by signposts such as other memories corresponding to experiences of the same time period.

Each of our experiences has left an impression within the mind. The organizing and positioning of the information in most cases has been automatic; it seems the mind has an inherent capacity for effective organization. But where are all these things being stored?

Imagine for a moment that your mind exists within a vast, nonphysical area or space. To a certain degree we are employing an analogy, because space as we know it is a characteristic of the physical universe and does not necessarily exist in the same manner within nonphysical dimensions. But focused as we are in physical reality, we have to employ images to which we can relate. Later, a better picture of the region of mind may become clear.

This mental space or dimension, then, is filled with energy of a nature far too subtle to be measured with physical instruments. Your mind occupies a specific region of this mental dimension, relatively separate from the minds of others. Author and clairvoyant Annie Besant refers to the mental body of an individual as being that portion of the self that occupies this region and is engaged in what we know as mental processes.[1] But whether we call it the mental body or our private mental space, it is still that region in the nonphysical dimension that comprises that which you know as your mind.

As we have an experience, a thought, or a feeling, the field of energy which fills this private mental space is impressed with patterns, vibrations, fluctuations, and currents. Fields within fields of energy patterns are set up and retained. And as we develop cohesive belief systems and conceptual patterns, each new experience is stored in that region of the mind to which it most directly relates, or in which the most closely associated experiences already exist.

As we mature, our mental space becomes virtually filled with a webwork of energy lines and fields, some of which store our experiences and some of which compose the structure of our beliefs and conceptual patterns. Some regions of this vast field of mental energy are immediately accessible to conscious awareness; other regions fade into the background and essentially become a portion of that which has been called the unconscious or subconscious mind. And other regions contain our operational structures—the constituent parts of our operational system—which we seldom scrutinize directly, but which nevertheless are engaged almost constantly as we relate with reality.

Eventually our operational mental structures serve to sort and categorize all new experiences. They assimilate each fresh experience in relation to the memories of past experiences and in relation to current personal beliefs, and this enables us to operate quickly and efficiently in the world we know. When you turn a corner and see a tree, you don't have to stop and wonder what that is that stands before you. You have seen trees before and you have mental energy fields with which you can compare this object and thereby immediately recognize it. Furthermore, you believe in the consistency of physical reality, and so you believe that the tree you see is indeed a tree and not a hallucination or a trick of reality. In a similar manner, you don't have to put your hand in a fire in order to know that it is hot; you have experienced the heat-giving nature of fire before, and you have a mental gestalt in your mind-space that contains or incorporates your previous experiences with fire.

So long as we are focused within a physical form, this mental space and the webwork of mental energies which fills it interpenetrate and connect with the physical brain. The brain, as science tells us, is filled with electrical charges, waves, pulsations, and sparks. In this context the brain may be seen as a translator of energies. As we perceive things through the physical senses, for example, the brain translates the perceptions into energy patterns which are sent to the mind. Conversely, the energy fields of the mind are available to the physical body by way of the brain's translating abilities. Portions of the brain, therefore, stand at the threshold between physical and nonphysical reality.

It would seem that the mind hovers about the brain but is not contained by it, but though this is a convenient picture of the mind's location, it is incomplete. The body and the mind exist in two different dimensions, and the spatial location of the body is relatively insignificant to the mind. From our point of view, it appears that the mind must be where we physically stand, but from the mind's point of view "here" and "there" are essentially the same.

You may gain some insight into this by considering out-of-body experiences (OBE) and dreams. During such experiences the mind may focus in regions of reality independent of the body's location while still being connected to the body. Therefore, although connected to the body, the mind is not limited by the same spatial restrictions as is the physical form. This concept will be made more clear when we investigate the multidimensional characteristics of mind.

So, all of our thoughts, feelings, mental constructions, and memories occupy places within the private mental space which exists within the context of the nonphysical, mental dimension. As we have already seen, they interconnect and interact not only according to the arrangements we choose to impose, but also according to their own inherent natures. The result is a matrix of mental energies which serves not only to give us a coherent picture of reality, but also to give us guidelines by which to operate.

This is a partial view of the mind as seen from the perspective of our focus in physical reality. Now it would be helpful to look at the mind from another direction.

CONSCIOUSNESS, SELF, AND MIND

Although it is not my purpose in this book to delve into the nature of self and identity in relation to consciousness, it nevertheless will be useful to look briefly into these issues to gain a better understanding of the relationship of mind to consciousness. I believe that the fullness of who and what each of us is cannot be expressed or manifested within the physical dimension, or through what we know as the private self. *What* we are in our fullness is a vast gestalt of consciousness, an immeasurable field of energy that is aware. At this broader level of our being, *who* we are may best be called the Self, with a capital *S*. This term—the Self—represents the fullness of our identity as it exists in the greater context; it is that which we strive to realize in our spiritual disciplines and endeavors. You and I as we now know ourselves are but partial expressions of this total Self; and our current level of awareness—our current scope or range of consciousness—is likewise but a partial expression of our total range of consciousness. We are more than *what* we presently realize ourselves to be.

In order for this vast field of awareness, our Self, to experience any particular, relatively limited dimension of reality, it must focus a portion of itself in a manner suited to the environment it is experiencing. It can project only a portion of itself into a particular dimension since no single dimension of reality is capable of holding or expressing the Self's full nature. And just as this greater consciousness will not "fit" into a particular dimension, our physical dimension for example, likewise the full identity of this consciousness—the Self—will not "fit" into the physical dimension. A limited amount of the Self, or greater identity, does, however, accompany the narrowed focus of consciousness on its particularized dimensional journey, and this relates directly to what we know as the self, the ego, or the "I." In other words, we also are more than *who* we presently realize ourselves to be.

Now, regardless of the nature of the dimension of reality in which consciousness operates or with which it is engaged, it needs a tool for interrelating. As said before, unmodified consciousness is simply aware energy (with, of course, the impetus towards expression). In order to operate actively within any reality system, consciousness must be able to gather experience, store it, assimilate it, and interact with the components of that system. The tool which our consciousness manifests and uses for these purposes is the mind. From our perspective the mind performs various necessary functions, including the storing of information, assimilation, reflection; it performs these functions under the guidance of the self, which in turn operates under the guidance and impetus of the Self.

The personal matrix of mind, therefore, is the filter through which consciousness relates to its engaged environment. The focus of our consciousness that is specifically attuned to the physical dimension must come to understand the laws and principles according to which the physical system operates. And it must maintain a sense of self as a focal point around which to gather experience. This sense of self—the focal point of identity—is, once again, what we know as the ego. By employing the processes of mind, consciousness ceases to be merely an observer and becomes instead an active participant with a functioning translator—the mind—and with a focal point of identity—the ego or the self.

The mental webwork of belief systems, thoughts, and feelings, therefore, serves as a screen through which consciousness views a specific aspect of reality and through which it receives new information in the proper context. The particular overall field pattern which is your mind becomes, in essence, the operator.

The ego serves as the navigator in the physical dimension, but it cannot navigate without the operational framework of the mind. In each dimension of reality our greater Self—our total consciousness—adopts an appropriate sense of self or identity as the navigator, but there is always an aspect of mind to provide the operational framework. The dreaming self, the identity which you maintain when you are engaged in dreaming, is an example of an alternate navigator. While dreaming, your sense of self changes: you do not retain the same memories as when awake, or the same psychic affiliations, but you are still the same Self—the same overall gestalt of consciousness.

The physical body serves as yet another tool—a tool, as it were, of the mind and self. The physical body has senses which allow it to register stimuli from the physical environment, and a brain which relays the information to the mind. Also, the body allows consciousness to manipulate within your physical environment and directly engage it, enacting the decisions which are made in the mind by the self. So the flow of information and energy runs in both directions—from unmodified consciousness to the body and the physical environment, and back from the environment through the physical senses all the way to the aware energy that is our overall Self.

It is the nature of consciousness to expand through the gathering of experience; it is the function of the mind to serve as the harvester. And it is the nature of the body to operate within the physical environment, thereby serving as a tool of mind, self, and consciousness. Thus the mind may be seen as a complex tool through which our consciousness interacts with a reality system, while at the same time being a partial expression of that same consciousness. Later I will discuss how this process takes place in reality systems other than the physical.

THE MIND'S LOCALE

Now that the analogy of the mind being a vast space filled with energy patterns is established, it must be partially dismantled. Space and linear time are parameters of our physical system of reality. Neither of these parameters defines or rules nonphysical reality, which is necessarily the region inhabited by the mind. Or at the very least, the space and time that operate within nonphysical reality are different from those that operate in physical reality.

If the mind occupies no physical space, then where is it? And where are all the energy patterns which fill it? In fact, where is this mysterious nonphysical dimension?

These questions in themselves betray a prejudice: inherent in the word "where" is a fixation on the concept of three-dimensional space. In relation to our environment, the nonphysical dimension is everywhere and nowhere. It does not matter where you are on the earth—your mind is still in the nonphysical dimension. It does not matter whether you are dreaming or out-of-body or travelling at the speed of light, you still stand at the same threshold to the inner dimensions.

Science is beginning to see evidence of this nonphysical reality through their investigations of subatomic particles. In the physical world nothing can go beyond the speed of light—to do so would involve breaking the theoretical barrier of time. But relativity and quantum mechanics not only entail the probability of dimensions transcending this speed barrier, they also provide evidence for it.

If something is able to travel faster than the speed of light, then according to our view of reality it would be able to travel from one place to another before it left! Distance could be traversed instantaneously. Scientists are beginning to describe the dimension in which such things take place as a "nonlocal system." Physicist Nick Herbert, in discussing the experiments of the Irish physicist John Stewart Bell, tells us that the principles of quantum mechanics call not only for the existence of a reality system in which objects and communications may travel faster than the speed of light, but also a system in which two different objects, once having been in contact, may affect one another without an intervening medium and irrespective of what we call spatial separation.[2]

Author Michael Talbot tells us that a characteristic of a nonlocal reality system may involve information being passed from one "place" to another, not through any intervening space, but through what may be termed "dimensional holes." He extends this concept by discussing the possible nonlocal nature of consciousness: "This ultimate nonlocality of consciousness in the universe is perhaps why it is so difficult to pinpoint precisely where consciousness is located in our biological brains. For if the what of consciousness is that it is pure information, in a meaning universe the *where* of consciousness becomes alternatively *no*where and *every*where. In a universe that is infinitely interconnected, conciousness can be anywhere it wants to be—in the dance of neurons in our brains, in a disembodied poltergeist, drifting lazily over a lost library book in one's own backyard, or zooming down over a nature reserve outside of Stanford, California."[3]

The current relationship between physics and nonphysical reality is covered more thoroughly in a later chapter. What is important to recognize here is that even physicists are beginning to glimpse a dimension of reality which is not limited by the rules and laws that govern ordinary physical reality. They see evidence of a dimension in which communications may take place not over the span of distance and time, but instantaneously through dimensional doorways. And they are beginning to see that we cannot define the location of consciousness and mind in terms of the reality with which we are familiar.

Therefore, we cannot begin to understand the location or the nature of our minds so long as we confine our thoughts to those concepts which demand that things must exist in some physical place. The mind and all of its swirling energies exist in a dimension that occupies no space as we know it. And the matrix of energies discussed previously does not have to be spread about over any distance, requiring associated thoughts to travel in order to make their connections. The dimension of mind allows for communication between various mental gestalts with no consideration of separation; they may reach each other instantaneously through dimensional or interdimensional doorways.

The analogy of the mind occupying a space within the mental dimension, though useful, cannot be taken too literally. You can really travel through endless corridors within your mind and never go any*where* at all. Consider telepathy. Frequently individuals report being aware of another person's conditions or actions as they are taking place, even though they may be separated from that person by many miles. Your mental energies do not have to fly through the air to reach someone else—they can go from here to there instantly.

Likewise, you may enter into your own mind at any point. It will always seem as if you are entering the mental realm from the same place, and in a way you are. But from that one place all mental "places" are equally accessible.

Because it is so difficult to discuss nonphysical reality, it is necessary to return to the analogy of mental space. We are limited by our conceptions and by the laws governing the reality in which we are primarily focused. Personal explorations of the mind and of the domain in which it exists will familiarize you with its nature far more than words can, since they rely strictly upon linear time and three-dimensional space. As long as we remember that we are using analogies, we may avoid the trap of letting literal interpretations interfere with our abilities to understand what is sometimes a very foreign dimension.

Mental Space: Private and Public

As is well known, not all of the mind's contents are immediately available to or accessible by the individual. The mental patterns and structures with which we primarily identify are those which are available to our conscious awareness. However, psychology has shown that there are portions of the human mind which have an operational influence on the individual but are not easily accessible to one's conscious awareness.

The total private mental space contains all of the energy patterns pertaining to the experiences, thoughts, and feelings encountered or entertained throughout one's lifetime. Your mental space contains all of the idea patterns, emotional patterns, and memories which are yours alone. Likewise, it contains all those beliefs which are unique to you and which serve as the operating principles for no one else; although others may entertain and engage similar belief systems, and they may even have shared some of your experiences. Still, the particular ways in which you organize your beliefs and your attitudes are unique. For all practical purposes, this private mental space is accessible to no one but yourself, except to the degree to which you share the contents of your mental space with others through some channel of communication.

Now, this private mental space must necessarily deal with great volumes of experience and information. It must also handle all of the mental functions such as thinking and assimilating. If at all times we had to keep every memory, idea, feeling, and impression within our conscious awareness, we would find ourselves unable to operate effectively in our reality. We would be so overwhelmed with the volume of information available to us that we would find it difficult to deal with the particulars of our moment-to-moment existence. We would be unable to maintain that fine focus of consciousness that is necessary in order to make the decisions and initiate the actions that are required in our daily lives.

Fortunately, many of our experiences and mental functions are carried out within portions of the mind which psychologists have defined as "the unconscious." As our attention is demanded for ever new experiences, we allow the events and impressions of the past to fade from our immediate view. Other events and memories are filed deeply within the mind simply because we choose not to remember or dwell upon them. Often our beliefs also seem to slip imperceptibly into unconscious regions, although with a little effort we can bring them into conscious awareness. In fact, all of the experiences and memories which are stored in these unconscious regions may be accessed under the right conditions, as experiments in hypnosis have demonstrated.

Therefore, not only do we have a private, conscious mental space; we also have a private, unconscious mental space. Both of these regions of the mind have their resident energy patterns and energy fields which serve as mediators between consciousness and the environment or reality system in which we are operating. There is, of course, a constant interchange of mental energies between these two private regions. We are always both sifting more into the unconscious and drawing from the resident patterns in the unconscious. From a psychological point of view, there are times when it becomes necessary to uncover unconscious material in order to resolve complexes set up in the past that have come to inhibit or limit the effectiveness of our relationships with reality. I will discuss this issue more thoroughly when I explain the personality matrix.

Closely impinging upon the private unconscious of each individual is the region of mental space which has been termed the "collective unconscious." This involves a thread common to all human existence; no matter how unique we are, we are all engaged in a common enterprise. We all share in the evolution of humankind and are all related not only physically but mentally. Furthermore, the human condition is a social condition. If we did not hold some agreement about the nature of reality, if we did not share a common world history, we would have social chaos.

How is it that we maintain our implicit agreement about the nature of reality? How do we manage this amazing feat of communication and socialization? It would be far too simplistic to say that this agreement comes about through physical communication alone. Of course, to a certain degree we do learn our language, history, and social behavior from others. But even the most uneducated or isolated individual retains a complicated bond with all others. A great portion of this bonding and connection takes place through the medium of the collective unconscious.

Psychologist Carl Jung first used the term "collective unconscious," and he considered it an inborn phenomenon. He said: "A more or less superficial layer of the unconscious is undoubtedly personal. I call it the *personal unconscious*. But this personal unconscious rests upon a deeper layer, which does not derive from personal experience and is not a personal acquisition but is inborn. This deeper layer I call the *collective unconscious*. I have chosen the term 'collective' because this part of the unconscious is not individual but universal; in contrast to the personal psyche, it has contents and modes of behavior that are more or less the same everywhere and in all individuals. It is, in other words, identical in all men and thus constitutes a common psychic substrate of a suprapersonal nature which is present in every one of us."[4]

The collective unconscious is a psychic or mental phenomenon which allows us to connect not only with the past of the species, but also with the present and future possibilities of the species. It involves mental energies and patterns which are shared by all people. As Leadbeater said: "There are vast numbers of thought forms of a comparatively permanent nature upon the astral plane [nonphysical reality], often the result of the accumulative work of many generations of people."[5] The collective unconscious is composed of vast mental spaces and structures which connect to and interrelate with all people. Portions of it may be brought into conscious awareness, and it serves, therefore, as a mental network connecting all people. Through it each may share in the realizations of all others. (This subject is dealt with in more detail in conjunction with morphogenetic fields and the group mind.)

There is evidence indicating that collectively we maintain what is termed a "consensus reality"—a picture or experience of reality upon which we all agree, but which may not accurately reflect the true or deeper nature of reality. In the West, recent discoveries in the field of quantum mechanics demonstrate that, in at least some situations, the observer of an event actually determines the nature of the event. As shown in Chapter 8, the mind has a direct influence on all that takes place around us. As author and psychologist Charles T. Tart points out in describing what he calls the radical view of the mind (a view which he does not necessarily subscribe to), "The idea, held in many spiritual systems of thought that have dealt with altered states of consciousness, is that physical reality is not a completely fixed entity, but something that may actually be shaped in some fundamental manner by the individual's beliefs about it. I am not speaking here simply of *perceptions* of reality, but of the actual structure of reality."[6]

Now, if we do indeed participate in some way in the ordering of our reality system, or at least in our agreed-upon perceptions of it, we must have ongoing inner communications. Even the most isolated individual enacts and relies upon the basic root beliefs in three-dimensional space and linear time. Even the youngest child perceives physical objects as reliably solid. These agreements and many others like them occur within the region of the collective unconscious, the collective mind. In this mysterious space we unconsciously confer with one another about our most basic perceptions of reality. There we also share information regarding our history and evolution, as well as our common purposes in human existence.

We also share what Jung called basic "archetypes."[7] There are symbols and images which hold deep and common meanings for all of us. When put to the test we all agree upon their basic meanings, hence the widespread development and use of mythological symbols. Clearly, there is a mental arena which is shared by all individuals.

So far I have discussed the private mental space, the mental space of the personal unconscious, and the arena of the collective unconscious. But the mind is still more complex than we have seen thus far. It reaches into dimensions and systems of reality of unimaginable wonder. Before we go into the ways in which mind transcends the physical reality we know, it is necessary to investigate the multidimensional properties of mind.

MULTIDIMENSIONALITY IN REALITY, CONSCIOUSNESS, AND INTERFACINGS OF MIND

Return for a moment to the concept of consciousness as your essential awareness. This consciousness and the mental energies which accompany it are able to focus in a wide variety of ways and into more than one system of reality. In *Dreamscape* I discuss the dreaming focus of consciousness and how it operates within the dimension in which dreams take place.[8] Reality consists of many dimensions, and certainly not all are physical. The dimensions to which the dreaming focus of your consciousness has access are nonphysical, and as already stated, some aspect of mind always accompanies consciousness.

Then there are your thoughts, obviously not physical. They are composed of nonphysical energies and inhabit a nonphysical dimension. The mind may engage the physical dimension through the medium of the brain and the physical body, but its basic existence is beyond the confines of the space-time reality we know so well. In dreaming and other altered states of consciousness, the mind and thoughts engage non-physical dimensions as easily as they engage the physical dimension in waking states.

When you close your eyes and imagine something or visualize an image, you are turning your focus of consciousness toward a nonphysical dimension. In out-of-body experiences you also sometimes engage nonphysical dimensions. Robert Monroe, an author and authority on OBEs (out-of-body experiences) tells us that during an OBE, "You can go into an adjoining room without bothering to open the door. You can visit a friend three thousand miles away. You can explore the moon, the solar system, and the galaxy if these interest you. Or—you can enter other reality systems only dimly perceived and theorized by our time/space consciousness."[9]

Finally, if you believe that your essential Self will survive death, where do you believe it will be? Certainly you don't expect that life after physical death will find you in physical reality. Evidence from nearly every direction points to the existence of dimensions other than the one in which we now primarily focus our consciousness.

As reality is multidimensional, so is consciousness. And where consciousness goes, mind goes also. Thus the mind serves as the instrument of interrelation in every dimension into which consciousness ventures.

Clearly, not all the information and experiences to which our overall consciousness is privy is readily available to our physical focus of consciousness. But it is beneficial, if not necessary, to understand that the mind engages many dimensions and that it has gained knowledge from all of its encounters. As you explore your inner mindscape, you will inevitably encounter information not obtained through the usual channels. The energy gestalts that carry this information can be just as valuable as those that carry the experiences of physical reality. Dreams are a simple example: you may learn a lot about yourself and reality through your dreams, though your dreaming experiences do not take place in physical reality.

All of the energy patterns of the mind interact. They are not compartmentalized in isolation from one another. Your dreams, for example, may affect the way you feel about yourself and your life. And certainly an OBE will affect your attitudes about the nature of reality, in both its physical and nonphysical aspects. So you cannot expect to understand fully the workings of mind unless you take its full range of experiences into consideration.

In the final analysis the best way to come to a deep understanding of your own mind is through direct examination and exploration. The best experience is personal experience, and all of us have more experiences available to us through our minds than we know. In the next chapter I discuss some of the ways in which we can and do directly perceive the nature and workings of the mind.

3

Direct Encounters with the Mind

Not a moment goes by that we don't use our minds in one way or another. While awake we are thinking, feeling, observing and assimilating. While asleep we create dreams and explore other dimensions of reality with the mind. Every action we perform engages the mind. Yet how often do we turn the gaze of our attention directly on the mind itself? How often do we stop observing and interacting with our external reality long enough to look within and investigate the nature of our inner reality? How is it that, though the mind plays a key part in all that we do and perceive, we rarely study our own minds?

Many believe that exploring the nature and contours of the mind should be left to philosophers and psychologists. Perhaps you think it is too difficult to explore your own mind. Or perhaps you think that the absence of objectivity implied in any self-exploration eliminates the possibility of true and accurate understanding. Maybe you even think that turning your gaze inward is unnatural, or perhaps unnecessary. But there is much to learn by examining our minds.

Your mind, with its resident beliefs, ideas, and feelings, determines your relationship not only with your world, but with yourself. Too often we establish an operational pattern within our minds, which then proceeds to function automatically. We come to believe something, and unless a revolutionary event brings about a change in that belief, do not question it but continue to operate as if it were true. We never stop to examine our own mental structures to see if somehow we ourselves are shaping or attracting our own experiences. We experience deep internal conflicts, but we seldom think to look within or endeavor to resolve those complexes for ourselves. Instead we often turn to psychologists, psychiatrists, doctors, ministers, or wise friends to resolve our conflicts.

No one is closer to your own mind than you are. No one has a better opportunity for understanding its patterns and machinations than you do. Others can only observe the workings of your mind indirectly; you can directly engage it, observe it, and change it as the need arises. And no one has a greater need for understanding your own mind than you. We cannot master our lives unless we master our minds, and we cannot master our minds if we do not personally examine them. As it is said in *The Tibetan Book of The Great Liberation,* "Without mastery of the mental processes there can be no realization."[1]

It is no great task to observe the workings of your mind. All it takes is the willingness to do so. Total understanding perhaps will never come, but to the degree that you unravel the mystery that is your mind, to that same degree do you increase your ability to live harmoniously and wisely with your world and with yourself. You may even find the key to the realization of your desires when you look within the mind.

The methods for exploring the mind are many. Each individual will find that some methods work better for him or her than do others. But the rewards and challenges are endless, and the way is open to everyone. Sooner or later we must all come to know ourselves and take full responsibility not only for our actions, but for our thoughts and feelings.

THINKING ABOUT YOUR THOUGHTS

Do you believe that you are at the mercy of your environment? Do you believe that you participate in the creation of your own reality? What do you think of yourself? Do you believe in God? Do you believe that you are tainted with original sin, or do you believe that you exist in a state of grace? Do you even know the answers to these questions?

Since we operate from the set of belief patterns resident in our minds, since those patterns are the foundation of all our relationships, isn't it imperative that we proceed from as true and as sound a mental foundation as possible? And how can you really know if you are operating from a sound mental perspective unless you know what that perspective is?

Ask yourself whether you feel your beliefs arose as a result of your life experiences. Or could it be the other way around? Did your experiences occur as they did as a result of your beliefs? Which comes first, the belief or the experience? It would seem that if our life experiences lead us to true beliefs, then sooner or later everyone would have the same beliefs about everything, which of course isn't the case. Perhaps you will find that beliefs dictate your experiences, and not the other way around.

It would seem that it is in our best interest periodically to examine the contents of our own minds. By simply asking yourself questions you can produce a list of your own beliefs and attitudes. Write down everything that you believe. Write down your thoughts about the world, about other people, and about yourself. This will require a good bit of thinking and no small measure of self-honesty, but you will discover a lot about yourself.

Once you have thought about what you believe, think, and feel, and once you have a good grasp of your personal perspective on reality, look deeper. Why do you believe that way? Are your beliefs based upon facts or upon suppositions? Do you have contradictory beliefs? If you do, then at least one of them must be unsound.

Most of us adopted beliefs in childhood as a necessary operational structure from which to begin our explorations of life. Many of us have failed to re-examine those beliefs with an eye toward determining whether they are still worth keeping. Sometimes we adopt new views and beliefs as we grow older, without throwing out the old ones which might be in direct conflict with the new ones. Such mental overlapping and unnaturally forced combining of belief patterns can lead to increasing conflicts as time goes on.

You do not have to be a philosopher to examine the contents of your own mind. All you have to do is ask yourself questions, think about them, answer them honestly, and be prepared to accept your own limitations and errors.

Do you desire money but believe that money is the root of all evil? Do you desire success but believe the world is against you? Do you think your essential nature is good, or evil?

We all have inner conflicts and contradictions. When we try to combine mutually exclusive thought patterns within our private mental space, we are setting the stage for inner conflict. An examination of your own inner mental structures will allow you to discover mental inconsistencies and false beliefs. Once you have discovered these, you are on the road to resolving your inner conflicts, thereby freeing yourself for more inner harmony and more effective action in the world.

Observe the tendencies of the modern person. Many spend their days working and their evenings watching television or reading. Have you noticed how few people are comfortable with quietude? If there is no activity going on, if there is no conversation, then there must be music or television or some other activity in which to engage the mind. Too many of us are afraid of being quiet long enough to hear the workings of our own minds. If you fear your own inner nature, or if you believe that your mind holds horrors and evils, then you will never examine yourself and learn the truth. But the longer we delay facing and examining our own thoughts and beliefs and feelings, the more do we allow inner conflicts and uncertainties to build.

We should not have to wait for crises before we proceed with self-examination. Once you are in the throes of a depression or crisis state, you are less able calmly and rationally to examine your mental state; by that time you are under the control of your immediate thoughts and emotions. The time to think about yourself, your life, and the contents of your mind is when there is no crisis.

If you do not know what questions to ask yourself in order to explore your own beliefs and thoughts, try some selective reading. Read some of the philosophers. You don't have to understand everything they are saying, but reading their works will raise questions in your mind. Read psychology works. Read the works of Emerson or Thoreau. There is a vast number of works that can give rise to important questions. By reading the works of various thinkers you will inevitably stimulate your own mind, and the questions will arise naturally.

Simple thinking aimed at self-examination is the easiest and most natural method for exploring the nature of mind. It requires no esoteric discipline, and it is not even considered "weird" by others. It exercises the mind and is a beneficial pursuit for everyone. Psychiatrists may be able to help us understand ourselves and resolve some of our inner conflicts, but you are the one who lives with your own mind at every moment. And you are the only one who has either the time or the interest in unraveling the full complexities of your own inner states. Also, you are the one who has the most to gain. Think about it.

MEDITATION

Meditation is the simple process of quietly looking within. It need not involve any sophisticated or esoteric methods. It requires no strange procedures or mysterious chants. It merely requires turning the focus of your attention in a direction other than the usual.

Most of the time our attention is turned outward. We engage the world we see through our physical senses. We think about what is going on from moment to moment, or we think about the past and future. In order to operate effectively in our world, we must pay attention to what we are doing and to what we are perceiving. But if we wish to understand our minds, we must occasionally look within.

In the first stage of meditation you sit comfortably, close your eyes, and begin to quiet the inner processes. The attention is withdrawn from the sights, sounds, and other stimuli coming from the external world. If you have never tried this before, you may find it more difficult than you would expect. Habit has accustomed us to pay relatively constant attention to what is going on around us. With your eyes closed, you will still hear all of the physical sounds that surround you. You will still feel a breeze moving across your skin. And you will still be aware of the sensations within your own body. But you must endeavor to ignore these things temporarily.

Once you are no longer paying attention to physical stimulations, what is left? Your own thoughts and emotions will next capture your attention. You may be thinking of all that has happened to you during the day. You may feel silly for attempting to meditate. You may be wondering just what you're trying to accomplish with your eyes closed. If you are aware of such thoughts and feelings more intensely than you're aware of your immediate physical environment, then you are already beginning to meditate.

It may seem to you at this stage that your efforts are accelerating your thought processes, but this may simply result from looking at your thoughts for the first time. As Ram Dass says, in speaking of meditation, "A common report is the feeling of the mind speeding up. Actually, this is not what is happening, but rather your awareness is standing back a bit so that for the first time you notice the normal speediness of your thoughts."[2]

At this stage simply be aware of what you are thinking and feeling. What is it you are thinking in regard to your job, or your family, or yourself? Do your thoughts jump around from one subject to another? Is there ever a pause in your thinking, or is it continuous? Can you control your thoughts, or do they come to you ceaselessly in a stream over which you have no control? What are the issues that occupy your thoughts?

A simple observation of the moment-to-moment working of your mind can tell you much. Many people are unaware of the ceaseless string of thoughts which occupy their minds. Even among those who are aware of the fact that they think continuously, very few are aware of the nature of those thoughts. Listen to your own mind. Is it chaotic, calm, directed, or worried? Attune yourself to your own feelings. Are you tense, sad, happy, or upset? Where is your mind and what is it doing?

You are now engaged in the first stage of meditation. You are simply observing the workings of your conscious mental energies. You are listening to your thoughts and noting your feelings. At this point you will likely find that your thoughts continually return to the situations and events with which you are confronted in your day-to-day life. You will likely keep thinking about what you recently did and what you intend to do in the near future. In fact, your thoughts will probably jump around to everything that concerns you, except for the immediate moment.

Now, from here you can take your meditation in several possible directions. You can continue to observe your immediate thoughts and then think about them. What kinds of attitudes and beliefs and feelings are you expressing about your job or your life? Why are you thinking those thoughts and feeling those emotions? Is this the way you want your mind to operate, or would you like to reorganize it? Simply observing your own thoughts and emotions and reflecting on them will do much to acquaint you with your own mind.

Another direction you can take at this stage is to attempt to quiet and focus your thoughts. Each time a thought appears in you mind, it is up to you to determine how much attention and energy you will give it. The more energy you feed into a thought or a group of thoughts, the more that particular mental pattern will be developed and extended within your conscious awareness. But if you withdraw your attention from a thought, it will quickly disappear from view.

Therefore, at this stage you may tell yourself that you are not going to pay attention to the thoughts that cross your mental vision. As a thought arises, just let it pass away. It may be useful at this point to pick one thing upon which to concentrate in order to keep your attention from wandering down the corridors taken by thoughts. For example, you might concentrate on your breath. Then, each time a thought arises turn your attention again to your breathing and let the thought disappear. Some people concentrate upon mantras; others simply concentrate on emptying their minds.

On doing this you will find that eventually your mind quiets considerably. Fewer thoughts intrude, and a feeling of calm and peace descends upon you. Relaxation and lessening tension affect both your mind and your body. However, there will still be thoughts, although less hectic, and the issues around which they revolve will change. You may stop thinking about your day-to-day life and begin quietly to contemplate more profound issues. By clearing your mind of the more superficial thoughts and emotions, you make it possible for deeper thoughts and feelings to show themselves. You can quietly reflect on some of these issues while you acquaint yourself with the deeper energies of your mind.

This process of inner observation, reflection, quieting, and deeper observation is the basic process of meditation. It is a very effective technique for acquainting yourself with the contents of your private mental space. Of course, there are different reasons for meditating. For instance, calming the mind is beneficial both psychologically and physically, since it relieves stress and rejuvenates the whole system. I have stressed meditation as a technique for observing the workings of the mind, since that is the basic topic of this book.

There is really no end to what can be learned or accomplished through meditation. One can explore the depths of the mind endlessly. With increasing stages of withdrawal from the physical realm, one's attention and conscious focus enter more deeply into the nonphysical dimensions, and aspects of reality transcending the private mind may be encountered. Deeper and deeper levels of one's own beliefs, thoughts, and feelings may be explored and understood.

As with any other method of self-exploration, the amount of time and effort invested depends on each individual. The rewards and discoveries will be directly proportional to your effort.

DREAMING

Beginning with Sigmund Freud and continuing to the present, psychologists have recognized that our dreams reveal much about our inner states. In *Dreamscape*[3] I discuss a number of different types of dreams, not all of which were purely subjective in nature. But those which concern us here are the ones in which we enact and encounter the workings of our own minds.

In many self-created dreams we directly confront our own thought-forms and desire-forms as they take shape in a nonphysical dimension. Our desires are unfolded before our awareness in vivid and complex forms. We "see" our thoughts as they take shape and develop into intricate scenarios. Our fears, hopes, and desires are enacted as dramas in which we often participate. Sometimes mental patterns which normally reside in the unconscious are brought to our conscious awareness.

If we recall our dreams when we awaken in the morning, we are often left with a confusing set of memories from our dreaming activities. Some of the remembered images are symbolic in nature, and some are fairly literal or straightforward in terms of the messages they communicate. The study and understanding of dreams can further help us to understand the patterns and workings of our minds.

Conflicts of which we are unaware in our waking lives may unfold before us in dreams. Problems confronting us in life may be faced and explored. Deeply buried traumas originating with childhood experiences may be recalled and faced. A wide variety of insights not available to us while awake may come as we dream. Learning to unravel our dreams will allow us not only to deal more effectively with life situations; it will also open greater avenues for exploring more facets of our own minds.

Previously I mentioned the ways in which thought-forms and mental gestalts gather and interact through association. Our dreaming focus of consciousness directly engages the mind's associational linkings. Most people are aware that many dream images are symbolic. These symbols appear to the dreamer according to the ways they associate with each other. For example, if you are facing feelings of vulnerability in a dream, you might find yourself naked in front of other people, the lack of clothing symbolizing your feelings of vulnerability. Or, to use the image of the rose again, you might dream of someone you know who is named Rose; or as a result of associated images you might actually recall the image of a rose from your dream.

This process of symbolic interaction through association reveals a key process of the mind's ways of operating. Furthermore, an understanding of your reservoir of private symbols and the meanings they convey will help you unravel the complexities of association which you encounter in your waking life. You might be able to rid yourself of an irrational fear of snakes, for example, if you know what snakes represent in your own mind. Or, by discovering your symbolic image for peace, you may be able to employ that image in your waking life to induce a feeling of peace when you are in need of it or in meditation.

I can discuss only briefly the nature of dreams, their meanings, and the usefulness of understanding them, since I have already written a book specifically dealing with this topic. The point to remember is that many of your dreams involve vivid manifestations of your own mental energies and patterns. They reflect your thoughts, feelings, beliefs, desires, and attitudes. Learning to interpret them gives you further experience with the mind's workings, and it aids in recognizing and dealing with the patterns of mental energy which you have established over the course of your life.

As said before, thoughts and other mental gestalts are composed of fields of energy of a nonphysical nature. In dreaming, you encounter some of these fields directly, perceiving them through nonphysical senses. You are still clothing them in images and forms which correspond to physical entities, so you are not seeing the energy fluctuations and currents in their primary state. But even wrapped in recognizable images as they are, while dreaming you are able directly to perceive thought-forms interacting, mixing, and associating in the mind. During some dreams you are actually inside your mind, watching the play of your own mental energies and processes.

At times through dreaming you may focus your conscious awareness into dimensions wherein you can see the energy patterns of your mind without the camouflage of physical images. Such work is only for one who is advanced in dreamwork, but I want you to be aware of the possibility of exploring the mind deeply and thoroughly through dreaming. If you are a beginning student of dreams, it is enough to become aware of the content of your dreams and to learn more about the workings of your mind through understanding dream symbols and events. Each method of exploring the mind allows a new perspective on mental energy patterns and currents.

IMAGINATION AND VISUALIZATION

An easy access into the realm of mind may be gained through the simple techniques of imagination and visualization. We have all had daydreams in which we close our eyes and let our thoughts drift off to another place or into fantasy. And though some would have us believe that daydreaming is a waste of time and involves no more than unreal phantasms, the fact is that the imagination puts us into a unique form of contact with the inner realm of mind.

Plato was perhaps the first to develop a theory of the imagination or, as he called it in its higher aspects, "phantasy." Author Murray Wright Bundy explains a critical aspect of Plato's view of imagination/phantasy: "Beyond Reason it is possible for human phantasy to go: impelled by love the poet may see in the beautiful objects of this world images leading one to think of Heavenly Wisdom; which, in this aspect, as the object of phantasy, must take the shape of Beauty. For neither Wisdom nor Justice nor Temperance, but that Beauty which is in all three is an object of vision. Thus Plato crowns his theory of knowledge with a theory in which the phantasy is recognized as the power by which the mind grasps truth made visible by the phantasy of God. Wisdom, Beauty, Love, and Phantasy: these are the terms involved in the Platonic doctrine of poetic inspiration. Wisdom is the goal of all though; Beauty its highest embodiment; Love the necessary restraint of impulse; and Phantasy the proper use of a power both of presentation and representation that the human may rise to the divine."[4] Thus we see that the imagination has long been valued by the wise.

Imagination and visualization involve the creative formation and attraction of mental gestalts. If we close our eyes and try to think of a peaceful place, images will appear before us which we associate with peace. If we daydream about success or wealth, we may visualize the splendor in which we would live if we had these. Or we may begin to see all of the things we might do with our hoped-for wealth.

Aside from the simple pleasures derived from using our imagination, there are more practical benefits that may be gained. We can create scenarios within the mind to help us in making decisions: in considering a new job, we might imagine ourselves in that new situation. Putting ourselves there imaginatively allows us to sense the feelings and thoughts that would arise in that situation. Without even noticing it, we frequently use imagination to explore possibilities, to initiate creative endeavors, to exercise our psychic powers, and to play.

Obviously we can use the imagination to observe the

associative connections within our private mental space. Close your eyes and think about fear or happiness or security. Immediately a series of images will begin to pass across your mental vision. The energy patterns corresponding to experiences you associate with such feelings will automatically be drawn into your conscious mind, your original thought serving as a magnet for them. Whenever you think about anything, through imagination you can enter into and observe the energy linkings within your own mind.

Not all imagined scenarios are constructed consciously. When we initiate a daydream or fantasy scenario, we don't really know where it will lead. Images and feelings will arise that surprise us and carry us along unexpected mental corridors. We may set up the original conditions, consciously establishing a mental energy field, but often processes within the mind take over and serve us in unexpected ways.

By using the imagination, we can unravel some of the mysteries of our own minds. Do you know what you fear? Try closing your eyes and setting up the vibrations of fear within yourself. Then watch for images that cluster around your emotion of fear. Do you know what kinds of situations make you happy? Induce the feeling of happiness within yourself and see what kinds of settings your imagination presents to you.

The imagination no more involves hallucinations than does thinking. It is a way of observing and working with mental energy patterns by activating your powers of visualization. You are either creating or drawing forth mental energy patterns that correspond and associate with your moment-to-moment states of mind. You are letting the mind furnish the drama which portrays your own inner desires, fears, thoughts, emotions, and beliefs. Imagination allows you to work consciously with the contents of your own mind, to explore your own self.

Imagination and visualization can also be used to change negative feelings. Are you sad? Try closing your eyes and thinking about images that you associate with happy times. As these images appear, they will evoke the emotional energy patterns you felt during those happier times. You will be creatively pulling positive emotional energies into your conscious mind where they will supplant the negative ones that have their hold on you.

Do you feel that you are too timid? Each day take a little time to imagine what you would be like if you were more aggressive or assertive. Imagine yourself as you want to be. By this process you will establish new energy patterns within your own mind, constructing new operational mental structures. In time these new patterns will actually begin to affect the way you operate in your life. Using the imagination, you can literally change your own psychological make-up so that you become more the person that you want to be.

Imagination and visualization can also be used to bring about changes in your life situation. I discuss this issue more thoroughly later, but I will mention it briefly here. The energies that form mental patterns have effects beyond the mental dimension. All things in reality are interconnected. In subtle ways your thoughts play an important part in determining which events and situations manifest in your life. Just as thoughts magnetically draw other thoughts and feelings, so do they also subtly draw events into your life. Therefore, through the creative employment of the imagination you can alter, and to a certain degree determine, the nature of the events that will transpire in your life.

Finally, you can use the imagination to enter more

deeply into nonphysical realms. For example, you can initiate OBEs with the imagination. If you close your eyes and vividly imagine that you are somewhere else, you begin to transfer your conscious focus from your physical body to your "traveling" body. With some experience in using the imagination, you might be able to enter the deeper levels of the mind and perceive uncamouflaged mental energies. The imagination can be used as a doorway into other realms: where you go when you pass through the doorway depends on your own powers of imagination and your beliefs.

The imagination is but one more way to enter the mindscape. We can use it constructively and learn much from it. We can observe our mental processes and change them constructively. Imagination provides a method for consciously manipulating the very energy patterns which reside in our private mental space. Therefore it can serve us in our efforts toward further self-exploration, self-realization, and enjoyment.

CREATIVITY AND INTUITION

Creativity is often closely linked to the process of imagination. Whether or not visual images are employed, artists and other creative individuals must turn within to explore mental channels in order to bring forth something new. Painters often visualize their works before they ever apply the brush to canvas. Some musicians compose entire works in their minds before transcribing the first note. Writers must explore different paths of expression within their minds before the words appear on paper.

In essence, creative products are not composed of original elements: most are the result of new combinations of familiar elements. The painter does not create new colors, and seldom does the writer create new words. Instead they juggle and mix the familiar until they are able to arrange a new ordering of elements, a process that is mental before it is physical.

Of course, some creations involve the conscious and deliberate manipulation of mental gestalts. Such experimentation inevitably leads to the occasional unique mental gestalt, and a new creation is born. But many creations come about in a different manner.

Anyone who is involved in the creative process sometimes must wonder where new ideas and conceptions come from. Insights seem to spring from nowhere. Story lines pop into one's head unbidden. The image of a painting suddenly appears before the mind's eye. In fact, many creative individuals have spoken of being but the instrument of the creative process rather than the sole originator of a creation.

Whether we are conscious of it or not, the mind interfaces and touches upon multiple dimensions and reality systems. The creative process involves attuning to normally unconscious portions of one's own mind. Or it involves the mind's ability to access information and realms that lie outside of one's own mental space. Or both. In such situations the individual is inevitably presented with the new. Creations are born from dreams. Insights are gained through deep meditation. And through imagination the awareness travels along new corridors. The mind is not a closed system; every mind intertwines its energies with reality in an infinite number of ways and through in infinite number of channels.

So sometimes the creative process involves bringing into conscious awareness information from one's unconscious contact with other dimensions of reality. Our private mental space, as previously mentioned, is in contact with the public mental space, and therefore to some degree we may mentally absorb the new through our nonphysical contact with everyone else. And who can say what other dimensions and beings are in contact with us through the hidden corridors of the mind?

Everyone has experienced intuitive flashes, insights which seem to come from nowhere, independently of the rational or reasoning process. Sometimes they may result from unconscious resolutions of previously un-assimilated information. At other times they may orig-inate from outside of ourselves, reaching our con-scious awareness through mysterious corridors of the mind.

Non-rationally achieved awareness and discovery, whether from the creative process or intuition, implies that we have access to mental experience via chan-nels other than the purely physical. Engaging in the creative process or attuning ourselves to the intuitive faculties brings us closer to these channels and allows us better to observe what is going on. Just as we gen-erate streams of energy as we think and feel, so do we entertain streams of energy when we create or in-tuit. If you can turn a portion of your attention upon the mind's activities while engaged in the creative pro-cess or while intuitively receiving insights, you can perceive these new streams of mental energy. Some-times you can even follow them in reverse, in order to find the source of the information, or at least to find the point at which the information enters your private mental space.

All of us have creative and intuitive abilities and moments of inspiration. When these moments are upon you, attempt to look within and "feel" the flow of mental energies passing through your mental space. This offers yet another method for exploring the reaches of our own mind.

In the deep recesses of mind we are all connected

and in communication. Information flows continuously among all beings at some level. Exploring your own mind will inevitably lead to an exploration of the nature of reality itself. And it will lead you to discover that you are always more than you think you are.

ALTERED STATES

Any time our focus of consciousness is turned in a direction other than what is most common, it may be said that we are in an altered state. As Charles T. Tart says: "For any given individual, his normal state of consciousness is the one in which he spends the major part of his waking hours. That your normal state of consciousness and mine are quite similar and are similar to that of all other normal men is an almost universal assumption, albeit one of questionable validity. An altered state of consciousness for a given individual is one in which he clearly feels a *qualitative* shift in his pattern of mental functioning, that is, he feels not just a quantitative shift (more or less alert, more or less visual imagery, sharper or duller, etc.), but also that some quality or qualities of his mental processes are *different*. Mental functions operate that do not operate at all ordinarily, perceptual qualities appear that have no normal counterparts, and so forth." [5]

Though the term "altered states" has taken on some negative connotations, the fact is that we all engage in altered states regularly without even recognizing them as such. When we dream we are in an altered state. When we are in the throes of inspiration we are in an altered state. When we are in moments of deep reverie, it may be said that our focus of consciousness is altered from the habitual focus upon our external reality.

There are degrees of alteration brought about by turning our awareness in different directions. These states may range from deep thoughtfulness to ecstatic journeys into nonphysical dimensions. But no matter the depth or profundity of an altered state, each time we use our minds in a different way we are exploring new facets of the mind and of reality. Each of these explorations may provide us with a new perspective on our own natures; each may serve to give us a better understanding of the complexities and ranges of our own minds. And each allows us to observe and engage new streams and fields of mental energy.

At this point I would like to discuss briefly some of the less common altered states in which we may participate. It is not absolutely necessary to engage in them in order to explore the mind. But for those who want to explore the reaches of their minds and their consciousness as thoroughly as possible, these are invaluable paths for exploration.

Deep Meditation

I have already discussed the simpler stages of meditation. The same processes involved in them may be used to bring about profound alterations in one's state of consciousness. As your meditative state progresses, you are in effect traveling deeper and deeper into your mind and into nonphysical reality. Each level of the mind holds its own set of mental energy fields and structures. As one quiets the activity at each level, the focus of awareness moves to the next deeper level and encounters the mental energies there.

Through such techniques as one-pointedness of mind one may enter states of consciousness that are quite foreign to our everyday waking mind. The nature of the mental energies encountered may be such that they no longer appear in the familiar guise of personal thoughts and emotions. You may be able to perceive thought-forms directly, seeing their colors and patterns without the camouflage of familiar images. Or you may find yourself in direct contact with that vast energy which is the source and spring of your own self, thereby experiencing a revitalization and illumination of a profound nature.

Suffice it to say that through the technique of meditation the deeper levels of the mind may be accessed, observed, and appreciated. There are other possibilities, of course, such as using the doorways deep within the mind to enter and explore other dimensions of reality. All deeper discoveries and realizations are encountered through the corridors of one's own mind. Meditation is a valuable tool for achieving these ends.

Lucid Dreaming

Lucid dreaming is a peculiar type of dreaming that may be induced or may occur spontaneously. It involves realizing that you are dreaming. I discuss this phenomenon in *Dreamscape*,[6] and further information regarding it may be found in such books as Stephen LaBerge's *Lucid Dreaming*[7] and Patricia Garfield's *Creative Dreaming*.[8]

Many of our dreams are self-created, as mentioned earlier. In such cases our mental energies are manifested instantaneously as dream dramas. As explained before, these provide a unique opportunity to observe your own mental patterns.

Because you are self-aware during lucid dreams, you may get valuable insights into the patterns of association within your own mind. You may also initiate experiences that dramatize the nature of the mind's relationship with reality at various different levels. Or you may enjoy vivid imagery as you explore your inner mindscape, discovering its deeper layers and its doorways into other dimensions. You may encounter and explore the nature of the symbolic images your mind employs that influence the organization of and communication between your own mental energy fields.

Lucid dreams involve bringing more of your conscious focus to bear upon the act of dreaming and upon the dream environment itself. It allows firsthand observation instead of the indirect interpretation of dreams that morning memories allow. Like all other forms of inner exploration, lucid dreaming is unlimited in its possible applications.

Out-of-body Experiences

The phenomenon of out-of-body experiences (OBEs) is also discussed in *Dreamscape*,[9] and in many other books, including Janet Lee Mitchell's *Out-of-Body Experiences: A Handbook*[10] and Robert Monroe's *Journeys Out of the Body*[11] and *Far Journeys*.[12] In the words of Robert Monroe, "An out-of-body experience is a condition where you find yourself outside of your physical body, fully conscious and able to perceive and act as if you were functioning physically."[13]

OBEs can be an indirect method for studying the nature of mind. Generally speaking, during these experiences you are not directly encountering the mind's energies, but as said before in every facet of existence the mind is employed. The ways in which you interact with reality in any dimension may afford insight into the workings of the mind.

A key benefit to having an OBE lies in experiencing one's focus of consciousness independently of the physical form. When you have an OBE you realize directly that consciousness and mind transcend the physical form. Furthermore, at such times you are able to obtain experiential evidence for the existence of nonphysical dimensions. This in itself will dispel any doubts you may have regarding the existence of the nonphysical energies of the mind.

Shamanic Journeys

Shamans of many cultures regularly explore other dimensions of reality and of the mind through shamanic journeys. These may be brought on in a variety of ways, such as through drumming, dance, ritual, or drugs. In such works as those of Mircea Eliade[14] and Michael Harner[15] we learn that shamans in all cultures journey into what they call the "upper world" and the "lower world."

These shamanic journeys may be likened to OBEs in that they involve the individual in traveling into other dimensions while the consciousness is focused outside of the body. During such journeys one may also confront aspects of one's own mind. Fears may take on the form of nonphysical beings; one's own greater self may appear as a spirit guide. However, like OBEs, shamanic journeys are usually indirect methods of exploring the nature of mind.

All altered states involve you in using the mind and its energies in new ways. It should be obvious that the more experience we have with the mind's activities and ranges, the better we can understand its nature. If we limit ourselves solely to the activities of the mind as it deals with physical reality, we are ignoring much of its function and purpose. Altered states are "altered" only when we are unaccustomed to them. Once we become familiar with new ways of using the mind and of focusing our consciousness, then altered states become simply some of the ways we interact with our reality.

OBSERVING THE MOMENT-TO-MOMENT FLOW OF THOUGHTS

There is one more method for investigating the nature of mind which must not be overlooked. We have a continuous dialogue going on within our minds. At every moment of our lives we are thinking about something and entertaining some emotions, whether we are aware of it or not.

Watch the flow of thoughts and feelings within your own mind. Listen to what you are telling yourself throughout the day. The mind is constantly revealing its contents to you, and you have but to pay attention in order to perceive the nature of your thoughts, feelings, attitudes, and beliefs.

You determine your own state of mind by the mental energies you engage in and entertain. You create and rearrange mental patterns continuously. If you tell yourself throughout the day that life is miserable or that you are unhappy, you create your own misery or unhappiness. You establish and reinforce mental patterns and energy fields at every moment. Would it not be wise to know just what you are setting up in your own mind? This observation of the continual flow of mental energies and patterns is probably the simplest and the easiest method for learning what is already in your mind and what you are presently inserting.

The mind is an excellent tool, but it can also be a chaotic master. However, you alone are responsible for the patterns and structures within your own mind. You can train yourself to arrange these as you want them. You are constantly telling yourself things, and if you become more conscious of this process, you can creatively establish the mental patterns you desire.

If thoughts and emotions do indeed consist of energy patterns, then they affect not only ourselves but those around us. Therefore, this constant flow of mental energies should be responsibly handled so that we do not unwittingly transfer unwanted or negative mental energies to others. To understand this, we need to look more deeply into the objective reality of mental energies, their nature, and their uses.

Part 2

4

Mental Structures and Power

The mind is complex, and it grows increasingly complex with each new experience and realization. Those aspects we normally observe, though important, are but the surface elements of a vast, multidimensional inner reality. However, by looking deeply into these surface elements we cannot help but find our way into the deeper picture. Because our conscious thoughts arise out of the greater depths of mind, they must necessarily serve as pathways into the deeps.

The normally hidden powers and structures of the mind need not remain hidden. In fact, it is our destiny to unravel the deepest mysteries. There is no danger that the immensity of the mind will unexpectedly flood us or overwhelm us; at the same time its mysteries will not retreat from those who diligently search within. After all, our minds are part of us, and nothing can keep us from ourselves.

In learning to penetrate the recesses of the mind more deeply, we will begin with the obvious and move toward the hidden.

MENTAL GESTALTS AND SYMBOLS

When we communicate with others we use symbols. Words, pictures, and signs are the most common types of symbols we employ in this process. In a similar manner, we communicate with the deeper portions of mind through symbols.

When we perceive an object or experience an event, we do so, at least in the physical arena, through the medium of our physical senses. Our physical perceptions are translated immediately into symbols. When we see a tree, we don't put the tree into our minds; instead we form the mental image of a tree and attach to it the word-symbol "tree." But this is not the end of the process.

As we adopt or use a symbol, we set up and establish thought-forms and energy gestalts. In the case of the perception of a tree, we generate and arrange mental energy into a structure and vibration which, whenever it is accessed, will bring into our conscious mental space the picture and word-symbol for "tree." We do not consciously manipulate and structure the mental energies; unconscious processes are involved in establishing the necessary energy fields in accordance with the dictates of the conscious mind.

In the same way, when we draw on information stored within the mind, we do not consciously access the energy fields. These fields are indeed called forth as a result of our intent, but we perceive them almost always in symbols and images that camouflage the energy fields, and to which we can relate from the perspective of our physical focus. If we wish to communicate the information within these energy fields to others, we use physical symbols, such as words or pictures. The symbols become our handles on the unperceived fields of energy.

We are immersed in the environment that is our physical reality system. So long as this is the case, one of our primary purposes is to relate to that environment, and through our relationship to it to increase our understanding of ourselves and our reality. Therefore, our current focus of consciousness employs symbols and images derived from our experiences within this reality system. Since the conscious mind is engaged primarily with our physical involvements, it must use symbols derived from the physical; in other reality systems we use different symbols.

There are both private symbols and symbols common to all of us. Furthermore, each symbol generally has more than one meaning. The image of a king might symbolize authority and order to one person and tyranny to another. Personal experiences, concepts, and associations determine the way an individual employs any particular symbol.

We do not generally think of our thoughts as being symbols because we do not directly perceive what is behind them. Similarly, we do not recognize that words are symbols because they are so intricately connected with the meanings they convey. Nevertheless, behind the thoughts that we mentally see and hear are the fields of energy that carry the primary impressions of our experiences. It is important to remember the distinction between the symbol and the energy field because when we investigate such things as telepathy, desire, and the controlled creation of mental gestalts, this relationship will be critical.

TYPES OF COMPLEX MENTAL STRUCTURES

There are several types of energy patterns within the mind. Each of these is closely related to the others, and the divisions, though convenient, are somewhat arbitrary. However, examining the types will help to make the structure of the mind more understandable.

Intellectual Structures

Certain complex energy patterns, like certain thought-forms, may be viewed as simple repositories of information. Mathematical concepts, logical sequences, and simple data are examples. When you register the simple fact that in your top dresser drawer are socks and underwear, you are simply processing and storing information. Similarly, when you memorize the multiplication tables you are storing information.

This type of mental structure may be likened to the memory banks or programming commands of a computer. A computer attaches no value to its information. It simply stores and organizes it in such a way that it is accessible when needed. The various different intellectual structures are quite numerous, and they vary in complexity, but the principle of the simple storage of information remains the same.

These intellectual structures are relatively static energy fields. They are the closest thing in the mind to a solid or unchanging structure of energy. By themselves they will go nowhere, unless we call them forth and set them into motion. They have no inherent magnetic properties.

Emotionally-Charged Energy Structures

When we add an emotional charge to a mental structure, new forces are set in motion. What was a simple, stable mental structure becomes a force field or an energy field in flux. Currents and polarities are activated, and the forces of attraction and repulsion come into play.

Energy patterns established by emotions cause mental structures to interact. On the simplest level you could visualize pleasant memories as being stored in one region and unpleasant memories in another. Of course this is an oversimplification, considering the complexities of mental structures, but the principle is sound.

Rarely do we have an experience that is not accompanied by some degree of emotion. Some experiences carry a high emotional charge and others carry a low one. Energy structures with a high emotional charge not only impinge upon more mental activities than those with a low charge; they are also more readily accessible to the conscious mind. We easily recall those experiences we felt strongly about.

Emotionally charged mental structures also play a stronger role in regard to operational patterns that affect your behavior or your reactions. If you have an unpleasant time at someone's house, you will be more likely to avoid that place than you would if nothing of particular interest occurred. Likewise, your reactions to different situations will to some degree be determined by emotionally charged mental patterns that relate to those situations.

Emotions and feelings are of many kinds. Value judgments partake of the same kind of active energies as do those feelings we normally call emotions. The value you place on information or experience contributes to the organization of your mental patterns. You draw on ideas, experiences, and beliefs you value and hold to be good, while those which you consider to be of little value recede into the background of your mind. Subjectively valuable beliefs and concepts are grouped together and become a part of your operational framework, and they determine what new experiences you seek out.

The magnetic properties and polarities of emotionally charged mental structures and gestalts also serve to draw new information and experiences into your mind through nonphysical channels. Out of the collective unconscious and other regions of the nonphysical dimensions, new ideas and concepts are attracted through the charges and polarities of these active mental patterns. Experiences related to mental patterns you value will be drawn to you; others will be excluded. For example, if you value telepathic communication, you will more likely be aware of instances in which it occurs; if you do not value it or believe in it, you will exclude the awareness of such instances from your conscious mind.

Emotionally charged mental structures are highly active. Unlike intellectual structures, they automatically play a part in what you do, believe, and draw to yourself. Their potency may be increased or reduced. They may serve to increase your fulfillment in life, or they may wear you down with conflicts. They are dynamic, and when I discuss controlled mental creations and desires you will see that they also are quite powerful.

Conceptual Systems

Conceptual systems may be viewed as a higher octave of intellectual structures. Philosophical systems, scientific formulas, and mathematical equations are examples of conceptual systems. Although emotional energies may be applied or appended to them, in and of themselves they are basically complex informational structures. The energy that composes them does not have the strong attractive and repulsive force of emotion, but they may serve as operational parameters.

Whereas an intellectual structure or information gestalt may be viewed as a simple, static structure, conceptual structures are like massive gridworks of relatively stable energies. They are composed of matrices of interlocking energies, but their currents and polarities are comparatively weak.

Structurally, these conceptual systems may exclude other thought-forms that do not fit their pattern, but this is not due to a repulsive force. If you have a conceptual matrix energy structure comprised of a set of scientific rules, for example, any assertion or information packet that does not fit into the structure of this system, that does not accord with its inherent rules, cannot be assimilated into the system. In a Newtonian system you cannot have relativity in the dimension of time, but in an Einsteinian system you can.

Similarly, although conceptual structures do not noticeably attract other mental energies, they do have parameters and forces that determine what may be added to them. A philosophical system that denies the existence of God would accept a proposition supporting a random universe. If you accept logics as the criterion of truth, then any logical statement will be accepted as valid.

Conceptual structures, like intellectual structures, may be made more dynamic through the imposition of emotional energies. However, when this takes place the structure essentially moves into a new category. We are then dealing with a system of belief.

Belief Systems

For us, probably the most critical and important mental energy structure is the one which composes our belief system. Our key operational framework is our belief system, and it is the most comprehensive system our minds contain, since it must serve as the primary intermediary between our consciousness and the world we experience. As author Beatrice Bruteau puts it, "To account for our total experience of seeking and finding contact with reality we must postulate both that there is a common ground beyond our individual and collective manipulations of experience and that our access to it is mediated by our conviction systems, the psychic grids." [1]

If you combine the matrix structure of a conceptual system with the charges, polarities, and currents that emotions bestow, then you will have a good picture of the energy structure of a belief system. Such a system involves a highly complex matrix structure that has all of the attractive and repulsive qualities of an emotionally charged mental structure, only these charges and currents are necessarily much more complex.

Everything we perceive or do is filtered through our operational belief systems. The currents, patterns, fields, and structures composing these systems affect every thought or feeling that comes to us, as well as our every perception. Our beliefs both limit and free our conscious awareness. They limit us to those experiences and mental patterns that agree with them, and they free us to experience and understand those things that fall within their range, or which that energy structure can support.

The subject of personal beliefs is dealt with more thoroughly in ensuing chapters, since it plays such an important role in our relationships with reality and in the nature of our personal mental patterns. For now, simply recognize that your general, overall mental patterns are organized primarily according to your system of beliefs. The field properties of this system govern your life.

POWERS OF CREATION

It requires energy to establish, maintain and operate the energy fields within the mind. When you choose to believe something, you use power to impress your mind with the energy patterns composing that belief. Thinking requires mental energy. Visualizing, imagining, sorting, and assimilating information—all activities of the mind—necessitate the use of some type of inner power.

The power to which consciousness and mind have access is truly infinite. It is the power of creation itself, the power and the energy that compose all that is. The only factor that limits your access to this power is the composition of your own mental energy patterns.

Spiritually oriented people often condemn the use of power for personal ends. But we cannot exist without power. Power holds the body together, and it enables us to move, think, and feel. Love is power; strength is power; and thought is power. The power of creation is the gift of the gods. Our access to this power gives us both great freedom and great responsibility.

What then is the nature of this power as it impinges on our private realities? How do we access it, and how do we use it? How does it affect us, and how do we affect reality when we employ it? Finally, what are the faces of this power?

Will and Intent

Each of us mobilizes energy primarily through the use of the will. Our attitude toward free will or determinism can affect this process. Believers in determinism assert that ultimately we have no power to choose, to act, or to believe; they contend that everything is determined by forces beyond our control and that at the most we are mere observers of the spectacle of life. Adherents to the doctrine of free will contend that we do indeed have the power to make choices, and that our actions can be and are determined according to our own volition.

Now, on the surface you may think that such philosophical issues have no practical bearing on your life. However, the question of free will versus determinism involves a basic belief pattern. If you believe that you are at the mercy of your environment, that events just happen to you and you can do nothing about them, then you are operating from a framework of self-imposed powerlessness. In such a case you are maintaining a critically important belief structure within your mind which holds that you are ultimately powerless to effect any significant change in your life.

Few of us clearly adhere to either the doctrine of free will or the doctrine of determinism. Usually there is a blending. You may believe that you are at the mercy of your environment, while still feeling that you can make small choices and changes within your life scenario. But to whatever degree you believe that the power that fashions your life lies outside of yourself, to that same degree do you limit your capacity for effective action.

Your will is your active power. It is your purpose and your intention set into motion. It is the directional mobilization of your consciousness.

Since we are multidimensional beings, our will, purpose, and intent operate at levels other than the physical. But for practical purposes I will discuss these from our current focus of earth-directed consciousness.

When you intend something, you activate your will.

You instruct it to set forces in motion in accordance with your intention. By intending something, choosing something, or deciding something you mobilize the energies at your disposal, and an inner process of implementation begins to occur. But, as we all know, our will and intent are sometimes thwarted.

Your will does not override your operational framework of mental energies. You may sincerely intend one morning to be more confident than usual during the course of the day, but if you strongly believe that you lack confidence, then your intention will be thwarted. If this operational framework were not there, we would find it much easier to effect change in our psychological structures: for example, we could change our attitudes about ourselves with the greatest of ease.

In the Gospel of Luke we read, "And I tell you, ask, and it will be given you; seek, and you will find; knock, and it will be opened to you." [2] Is this not another way of saying, "intend, and forces will be set into motion to accomplish your intent"? Your will is your power, and your mind governs that power.

Desire as Power

Your desires are diluted and masked versions of your intent. As mentioned earlier, your desires are mental structures with magnetic properties. In order to establish and maintain desires within your mind, you must employ your will to give them energy and to shape them. You must charge them. They grow in strength to the degree that you imbue them with increased amounts of energy through concentration, repetition, and emotion.

It should be easy to see the difference between the statements "I want that" and "I will have that." Willing carries with it a determination that is not present in simple wanting. When we want something there is often a degree of doubt as to whether or not we will get it. When we *will* something we bring more direct and more substantial energy to bear than we do when we just want it.

Attitude is another factor that makes desires weaker than concentrated intent. Desiring involves a longing for something that is seen as out of reach, or at least not present. Often when we desire something we concentrate on the desired object and also on the fact that we *do not* have it. Mental energy then becomes divided between wanting and believing that we do not have. It should be obvious that there is a distinct difference between the two approaches of desire and will.

Desires involve a blending of the will with the complex and manifold machinations of the mental matrix. Greater complications arise under these conditions. Competing desires, conflicting belief patterns, changing desires, and mental uncertainties entail a fluctuation of mental energies that makes the objects of our desires seem hard to attain. But as we shall see, there are ways to increase the likelihood of our desires coming to fruition.

Concentrated Mental Energy

Power may be concentrated within the mind in a variety of ways. Emotional energy intensifies desires, fears, and reaction patterns. But, as briefly mentioned, mental energy may be concentrated and intensified without necessarily employing the energy of emotion, though most energy patterns within the mind have at least a little emotional energy in them. Their subjective importance implies some degree of emotional attachment.

When we employ the will, to whatever degree, toward establishing or generating a thought-form, gestalt, or mental stream, we are applying power to the mental matrix. It takes some effort to think. Some thoughts seem to surface unbidden, but these are responding to patterns of energy and power that have long been in place. Somewhere along the line you introduce a pattern of thinking which continues on, partially as a result of the initial power and partially from the continued attention you pay to these surfacing thoughts.

Every time you entertain a thought and every time you give attention to an emotion, you increase its power. By attention you consciously direct your mental energies. You may address some problem, you may dwell on the image of a loved one, or you may impress your mind with the subject of a book you have been reading. Later, although you may be occupied with some other task, that subject or thought upon which you have recently dwelt, and in which you have invested so much attention, returns to you unbidden. It has, at least temporarily, gained enough power through your attention so that it is not far from your conscious awareness.

Most of the time the process of applying power in establishing and maintaining thought-forms and mental structures takes place automatically and with a relatively low level of conscious attention. Habitual patterns of thinking become ingrained to the point that at times we wonder how we could think in any other way. But once you become aware of what you are doing when you direct your attention toward particular thoughts and emotions, then you have the power to make dramatic changes. You are free to choose what thoughts and feelings you will entertain. You may imbue them with however much importance and power you think they deserve. And, as I discuss later, you may thereby have a significant effect upon the nature of your own experiences.

The power of a mental structure may be diffused and dissipated, thereby reducing or eliminating its influences in your life, or it may be increased, thereby giving that mental structure greater effectiveness. The will gives us the power to direct our attention, and attention focuses and funnels energy into and through the mind. We each have the power and freedom to direct the nature of our inner lives, thereby influencing our outer lives. Wise and discriminate applications of mental power can do more than move mountains.

So, how do we increase our personal power? How do we improve upon our abilities to order the mind's patterns? The infinite domains of reality obviously contain more power than we could ever need. Let's now take a look at the basics of accessing the power that surrounds.

ACCESSING POWER

Obviously, the power or energy which is tapped through the mind is not a physical power, but so long as we are focused in the physical arena it must make its presence known there. This energy which is at the disposal of the mind and the psyche cannot properly be said to belong to the user. It is the force of all reality—to be used responsibly, but never owned.

Power is neither good nor evil. It simply is. As with all things, its value comes with the nature of its application. I am addressing the tapping of power for several purposes: increased understanding; greater effectiveness in the management of one's own life, with an eye toward the betterment of all; and the attainment of a harmonious, fulfilling relationship with all of reality.

Marshaling Your Forces

The first key to accessing greater mental power lies in the proper use of what you already have at your disposal. As mentioned, every thought and mental pattern is composed of energy and is strengthened through attention and use. What is the nature of your personal mental structure? Is it an efficiently operating system?

If you have attempted to explore your mental state, perhaps through some of the methods mentioned in Chapter 3, you have probably noticed that your thoughts are scattered, and for the most part uncontrolled. One moment you may think about what happened in the recent past, perhaps dwelling on work that day. In the next moment you may think about what you are going to do in the future. From moment to moment your thoughts probably jump from one subject to another, with no apparent order.

And what about your beliefs? Do you have a cohesive, well-founded system of beliefs? Or do conflicting beliefs operate simultaneously? Do you even know what you believe?

Imagine for a moment a complicated machine. Imagine that this machine has some imbalance or faulty timing within the mechanism. When it is running slowly you don't notice the imbalances. When you speed things up a bit you begin to notice a vibration, or an inconsistency in its performance. Now imagine that you gradually add more and more power to this machine. As it goes faster and faster, the vibration increases. Soon it's bouncing and moving about. Finally it reaches a point where it has so much power and is running so fast that it literally shakes itself apart.

The more power that is put into a disordered system, the more apparent the faults and weaknesses will become. The mind may be compared to such a machine. But the mind fortunately is self-regulating and will permit no more energy into its system than the system is capable of handling. There are, of course, instances of overload, but they are the exception. Therefore, if you wish to increase your ability to access and use mental power, you must first tune the system so that it is capable of handling that power. You must make whatever adjustments are necessary to insure an efficient mental structure.

If your attention is forever scattered, then your current mental powers are seriously diluted. The first order of business is to exercise your powers of concentration so that you can bring the focus of your attention to one point and hold it there. It is the same principle as that of a magnifying glass that focuses the sun's rays. Focusing the light brings great power to bear on one point. With the mind the device used for focusing is not a glass, but the faculty of concentration, or attention directed by will.

Developing powers of concentration is equivalent to developing muscular strength. Anyone can do it; it merely takes exercise. The more effort and time you put into practicing concentration, the more your powers of concentration will increase. It does not take inhuman amounts of concentration to control your thoughts. It takes just a little more focus than what the habitually scattered and roving mind is used to. Many people are already able to concentrate for short periods and need only to stir up motivation.

Without the ability to concentrate, you cannot put

an end to those thought patterns that are injurious to you; nor can you implement new and beneficial patterns. Furthermore, if your attention is forever scattered, you have grown used to seeing your mental energies dissipated without achieving any significant effects. How much that you idly think about do you really want to think about? Some of your energy goes into the entertaining of those thoughts; if they do you no good, you are wasting your power.

You can act only here and now, whether in the physical or nonphysical arena. You can assess and calculate as a result of thinking about the past and future, but action must always be taken in the present moment. Marshaling your forces into the present moment increases your ability to take effective action.

Finally, it is critical that you assess your beliefs, and mental concentration will help you do this. Your operational parameters must permit you to expand your perspective and implement new beliefs. Your beliefs are self-fulfilling—you perceive what you believe—so beliefs are the principal key to your effectiveness and efficiency.

Restructuring the Mind

Once you have gained some proficiency in gathering your mental energies into the focus of the present moment, you can begin applying that energy to the task of mapping your mental matrix and making the necessary adjustments. The first and most practical place to begin is with your moment-to-moment flow of thoughts. Since your underlying beliefs, attitudes, feelings, and opinions are expressed there, that stream is clearly your first point of access to the deeper regions of mind.

When the opportunity arises, focus your attention

on the thoughts that come into your mind. You will need all of your available powers of concentration not only to catch the thoughts, but to hold them in your mental vision long enough to evaluate them clearly. What is it you are saying to yourself? What attitude or belief lies behind it? Does it reflect the kind of attitude you wish to hold? If it reveals a belief, what is the basis for that belief? Try to visualize that thought as an energy construction, and then rotate it and look at it from all sides. Is it connected to other attitudes, and if so, what are they?

Now if you decide, after careful analysis, that a thought or mental pattern is not of a character that you wish to maintain, then you must begin the process of either dispersing it or rechannelling its energy. In order to do this you must bring new mental energies to bear upon it; you must manipulate currents of power within your mind in such a way as to dismantle the structure of the thought which you are seeking to change.

The process of dispersion and rechannelling must occur on two levels. On the first level you deal with the surface thought itself. As you continue to hold the thought or pattern before your mental vision, think about why it is untenable or unwanted. If the thought has no firm basis in reality, explain to yourself why it does not. If it has a detrimental effect on your overall mental or emotional state, make that clear to yourself. If it is a thought which involves some negative attitude about the world, yourself, or other people, convince yourself that such a thought does no one any good. By exploring the untenability of a thought and by making its detrimental effects clear in your own mind, you are diffusing its power. If from a convincing, rational basis, you can firmly convince yourself that you do not want to entertain a particular mental pattern, you will be removing the support from that thought.

From a structural viewpoint, you are systematically cutting the lines of power which feed that thought-pattern. But this process must be done clearly and thoroughly. You must hold the thought-pattern in the grip of your mental attention and look at it from every angle, until you have found every line of power that feeds it and have effectually cut off those lines. Without these lines of force, the thought-pattern will lose its ability to continue, and the remaining structural energy will disperse. In this way you not only free the power which composes the structure or pattern; you also stop the flow of valuable mental energy into it.

Some thought-patterns do not require total dispersion. They may need only to be adjusted or rechannelled. If they are basically sound and useful but are slightly tainted with unwanted or negative energies, then you must cut only those lines of force that contribute to their negative side.

In other cases a thought may be sound and positive, but of little use. In this case examine why you are thinking about it at all. Is it because you are not thinking about anything else of greater importance and your mind just wants to be busy with something? Chances are that it is there simply because your mind is not more profitably engaged. If so, then all you have to do is remove your attention from that thought, or banish it from your conscious awareness.

If you find that you frequently entertain idle, useless thoughts, you may want to put your mental energies to better use. You can spend more time practicing your powers of concentration. Then you will employ the free energies of your mind for constructive purposes. Idle thoughts will dissipate; the energy that sustains them will be rechannelled and put to other uses. Or you might try exploring your idle thoughts to find their origin, and then cut them off at their source.

Some mental patterns, no matter how many times you cut off their lines of power, will resurface. If this is the case, you have an underlying belief pattern that is generating those mental patterns. Somewhere in your mental space you have constructed an operational pattern that is pumping out attitudes, thoughts, and feelings in accordance with that pattern of thoughts. For example, imagine that you believe you are basically worthless. From time to time during the day, you may discover a variety of thoughts that originate from this theme: you can do nothing right, no one likes you, other people are smarter or more capable than you. If you simply disperse the surface thoughts and do not attend to the underlying operational pattern, then those types of thoughts and feelings will inevitably return.

You cannot cut the lines of power from the surface alone. You must assess, evaluate, and restructure belief patterns. This subject comes up again and again because it is of primary importance. Your surface, conscious thoughts can and do give valuable clues to the nature of your beliefs. When those thoughts are of an undesirable nature, then they are a call to examine your beliefs and to make changes.

Changing beliefs is not easy. Because they involve operational patterns, they are imbued with a tremendous amount of mental power. They have been reinforced from minute to minute, possibly over the course of years. Much of your mental energy is invested in them, and much energy will be needed for their restructuring. But this cannot be done until you know their nature.

Once you have managed to gain a clear picture of an unwanted belief pattern, you have two things to do. First you must go through the process of making clear its untenable and undesirable nature. You must convince yourself that it is an operational pattern by which you no longer wish to operate, which has no value and is not sound. Second, you must replace that belief with one that deals with the same issue, but which addresses the issue from a direction you desire and is valid. In other words, you must replace a negative belief with a positive one.

Once you have convinced yourself of the undesirable nature of an old belief and have clearly shaped a new, positive one, begin to apply energy to implement the new belief. It is helpful to affirm or reinforce the new belief at least once every day. If you occasionally discover thoughts in your mind that reflect the old belief, then banish them and reaffirm the new belief. It takes time and energy to implement the new, but once it is accomplished it will effectively redirect enormous amounts of energy in your favor.

This exercise will likely begin as an intellectual one while your emotional energies still side with the old belief. To overcome this, act on the new belief. If possible, take some action each day that accords with the nature of your new belief. If, for example, your new belief affirms your sense of self-worth, treat yourself to something unexpected that you enjoy. Or assert your opinion in a situation where in the past you would have remained silent. In some way take action that expresses or affirms your new attitude. This will redirect emotional energies into the new operational pattern. Eventually the new belief will become self-fulfilling and will naturally reinforce itself.

Tapping the Power around You

Power and energy are everywhere, in everything. There is power in the storm that rages through the night, and there is a gentle, insistent power in the growing grass. There is power in the relentless surging of the ocean's waves and in the radiance of the sun. Can we, with the mind, draw upon such power? Can we draw upon the infinite, powerful resources which surround us?

Behind every physical force of nature there is a nonphysical force. What we perceive as physical reality rises out of an immensely powerful nonphysical reality. Just as we can physically transmute physical energies, so can we nonphysically transmute nonphysical energies. The key to transmuting and tapping these vast powers lies in identification.

We often place an imaginary boundary around ourselves and say: "This is where I end and there where the 'other' begins." But the self does not have to be so limited. The Self is boundless and there are no closed systems. Any limits to the self are arbitrary and self-imposed. Psychically we can reach out and identify with the forces around us. All things are connected. Each part of the whole depends upon every other part. In the last analysis there is only one of us, and that One has an infinite number of faces.

If you can allow your sense of self to be flexible enough, you can consciously realize and draw upon the connections that exist between you and all else. Have you ever stood looking out the window at a powerful thunderstorm and felt its exhilarating power within your own being? Have you ever looked at the starry sky and felt its immensity penetrate into your very soul? Such moments contain glimpses of the ways in which you can draw upon the power that surrounds you.

Accessing such power does not mean taking the power from some place and claiming it as your own. It means rather recognizing the oneness that already exists. It involves letting your self expand to encompass more than you knew yourself to be.

You must begin by believing that this is possible and that you are capable of realizing that possibility. And finally, you must make the effort. Employ your imagination. Attune yourself to your subtle senses and remember that you are dealing with nonphysical energies. Believe that the force with which you are identifying is filling your inner being.

You will never be able to understand the nature of the power that is available to you through this technique until you try it. The mind impinges upon and connects with nonphysical systems as thoroughly as the physical body connects with the physical system. Later I go into this topic, but for now bear in mind that you will be dealing with more than lifeless energy; you will also be dealing with the consciousness inherent within this energy.

A deeper understanding of the possibilities of this technique will develop if you look at the ways mental and other nonphysical energies interact. Also, you will better understand your own mental matrix by understanding the effects of your mental patterns on yourself and on others. The next chapter addresses this topic.

5

Effects of Mental Energy

It should be clear by now that thoughts and the fields of energy composing them can affect others, as well as ourselves. Energy affects energy; power structures influence other power structures. How does this process take place in the realm of mental energies? How aware are we of this process, and how can we become more aware of it? Can we benefit from the knowledge that mental energies have power?

INTERACTIONS IN MENTAL SPACE

Ultimately there are no isolated energies within the mental dimension. Just as a storm at one location in physical reality will affect the weather patterns miles away, so do the energy fields within one mind reach out to influence the energy fields of other minds. The same field interactions that take place within the confines of a private mental space also take place between the energy fields of different minds.

Each mental energy field affects and plays upon every other energy field within its range. Sometimes one enhances another and sometimes one interferes with another. At other times several mental structures may blend in such a way as to give rise to totally new patterns, which then give rise to what we call new realizations or revelations. An understanding of the nature of these far-ranging influences and interactions not only makes it easier to implement desired changes within the private mental matrix; it also makes it easier to bring about the most fulfilling reality scenarios for ourselves. Let's look at some of these field interactions in greater detail.

Harmonics and Mutual Compatibilities

It is the tendency of all things to grow, expand, and express themselves. A field of mental energy naturally gravitates to other fields that complement it and also naturally influences other energy fields whenever possible. It does not matter whether the energies under question are positive or negative, or whether they constitute truth or falsehood. All that is required for attraction or mutual influence is that the energy fields involved are similar in nature.

If there are two pianos in a room and you strike a note on one, then the string corresponding to that note on the other piano also vibrates. This is known as harmonic resonance. The same effect takes place within the mental dimension. How often have you been reading a book and come across an idea that seems to "strike a chord" within your mind? Are you not pleased when someone expresses an idea or opinion that agrees with one you hold? Similar mental patterns, whether within one mind or involving communication between two or more minds, stimulate and energize each other. We like to hear our own beliefs and opinions affirmed because it stimulates and reinforces them. It increases their strength and thereby increases the power that resides within our minds.

As mentioned before, within your private mental space, thought-forms and gestalts of energy of a similar vibration gather together. Each adds force to the others by increasing their amplitude through harmonic resonance. If you pluck a guitar string it vibrates; if you pluck it again while it is vibrating it vibrates more intensely, thereby increasing its volume. In the same way, mental energy structures of the same or similar vibrational rate continually reinforce each other, so that the whole gestalt increases in vibration and power.

Similarly, if without speaking you mentally concentrate positive energies on another person, that person will find his or her positive mental energies are stimulated. Our moods, emotions, and thoughts elicit similar energies in those around us. Likewise, the mental energies of others affect us through harmonic resonance.

Mental energies may stimulate one another through means other than resonance. When we are exposed to mental structures similar to our own, such as compatible beliefs, these reinforce our belief system. Similarly, when we experience an event that affirms what we believe, we eagerly impress our minds with it, since we perceive it to be evidence in support of our belief. In so doing we add power to our overall mental matrix, regardless of the relative soundness of the beliefs.

Each new concept that reinforces part of a general belief structure strengthens the whole structure. This process may be likened to the framework of a building—each new support beam reinforces the whole building and increases its structural integrity.

Interference Patterns and
Mutual Incompatibilities

Dissimilar mental energies repel and interfere with each other. From time to time we all have experienced mental confusion, unrest, or inner conflict. Any attempt to force two opposing or dissimilar beliefs to coexist within the same mental space is bound to cause conflict.

If two notes are struck on a piano at the same time, neither string vibrates as long as it would if it alone were struck. Differing wave patterns interfere with and dampen each other. In the mind, differing thought-patterns meeting can have a weakening or draining effect. If the mental energies which oppose each other are strong enough, or if they are important enough, their meeting may cause mental anguish.

This does not mean that all of our thoughts must be of the same nature in order for us to have mental peace. Different ideas and mental patterns are inevitable. But when there is an actual opposition or antagonism within fields of energy, the equanimity and clarity of the mental space is disturbed. This is especially true of incompatible beliefs.

Two opposing beliefs may cancel each other's effectiveness. You may begin to act upon one belief and find that another belief convinces you that such action is unwarranted. You may try to affirm your sense of self-worth, only to find yourself thinking of all the reasons supporting a belief in your unworthiness. Each belief or thought-pattern strives to maintain its importance and viability. If a mental energy pattern is threatened by another energy pattern, it may assert itself, making it appear as if dissimilar energies are attracting one another.

Why is it that discussions and debates so often turn into heated arguments? One answer is that when we hear an opinion with which we disagree, we feel a threat to our own viewpoint. Without a feeling of threat, we can counter opposing views calmly and with detachment. Emotional reactions to opposing views are a defense mechanism against what is perceived to be an undermining or weakening of one's own mental structures.

It should be clear that if you have an overpreponderance of any one type of mental energy, it is unlikely that your mind will ever permit opposing views to enter. This can be either beneficial or harmful. If your mind is filled with negative attitudes, it will be difficult to entertain positive attitudes. But if your mind is filled with positive attitudes, it will be difficult for negative ones to enter.

We also affect each other, often unconsciously, through mental interference. While our mental energies attract harmonic resonance from the minds of others, they also repel dissimilar mental energies. Of course, each individual has the power to choose the mental energies he or she will entertain; people with strong mental power will not be affected unwittingly by the thoughts of others.

Finally, awareness of inner conflicts means you are entertaining conflicting or dissimilar mental energies. Our available mental power is reduced when we force the mind to hold conflicting views. The energy is expended in the constant sparking and agitation that occur when highly dissimilar mental patterns coexist. A preponderance of such mutual incompatibilities may lead to severe mental crises. But we can find a way to resolution and harmony, and thereby enlarge our mental structures.

Associations, Blendings, and New Wave-Forms

Generally, mental patterns are neither totally alike nor totally different. Usually there is a blending of similarities and dissimilarities. When this occurs, we have the normal stimulations of an active mind. Minor dissimilarities challenge the mind, and the similarities strengthen its structural integrity.

Some mental patterns may be similar at one point and dissimilar at other points. In such a case they may have a line of force connecting them, but will not cluster together under the same umbrella, so to speak. Such a situation may or may not elicit the need for a resolution.

The interplay of these mental energy fields is not structured as rigidly as it may seem. There is constant motion within the mind; thoughts interweave, interact, move apart, and move together again. New ideas and patterns are compared with old ones, and continual adjustments are made. Decisions call for all relevant patterns temporarily to come together, be compared, and interrelate. There is a constant flux within the mind.

As thought-patterns merge and interact, new patterns and energy waves are set up. Thus we may come up with a new idea as a result of having considered, in conjunction, a number of known things. Unexpected revelations or realizations may occur when seemingly dissimilar energy fields are combined. We are always seeking new experiences and new information, even though we risk it not fitting with our already established notions regarding the nature of reality. Unless artificially inhibited, the mind always knows that there is more to understand, and it is therefore continually experimenting within itself in its attempts to grow and expand.

This blending, mixing, and comparing is the essence of mental growth. It allows for change, not only in surface thoughts, but in our operational belief structures as well. Flexibility, or the openness to consider diverging viewpoints, permits us to expand our perspectives. Thus, the mind evolves naturally toward cohesiveness and operational effectiveness. Therefore, a certain amount of mental churning and blending is necessary.

TELEPATHY AND THE HIDDEN INFLUENCES OF MIND

Whenever we speak of harmonic resonance or interference taking place between one mind and another, we are speaking of a form of telepathy. Telepathy, in the general sense, may be described as any communication that takes place between two or more individuals through extrasensory means. It need not involve only the conscious transmission and reception of thought-forms. Since so many of the activities of the mind are hidden from our view, it would be naive to assume that none of those hidden activities involves our communicating with others. As we saw earlier, communication through the collective unconscious is one example of telepathy, albeit indirect.

Just as we do not witness the full range of effects our physical actions bring about, neither do we witness the full range of effects of our mental energies. When you walk into a room full of happy people and find your own spirits lifted, you may not realize that this is partially due to telepathic communication. Likewise, when you think about someone on a particular day and then that person phones you, you may consider it coincidence. We do not recognize that communication with others through the mental dimension occurs all the time; we have trained ourselves to ignore it. There comes a point, however, when we need to become aware of the effects our thoughts and emotions have on others. We also need to know how others' thoughts and emotions affect us.

How far are thoughts projected? What governs their direction? These are questions for which we need to know the answers.

Mental Influences through Subjective Proximity

Obviously, the people around you physically are most affected by what you do. Since they are closest to you, your actions reverberate outwards and influence their lives. In the same way, your mental energies have their greatest effect upon those with whom you have a close psychic relationship, generally the same ones with whom you have a close physical relationship.

You think about the people you know and have feelings about them. Therefore, you have mental energies which specifically relate to those people. Some of these patterns and energies are consciously directed towards others, as when you think and feel "I love him," or "I hate her." Others are directed unconsciously, as when you idly think about someone and wonder what he or she is doing.

So long as you do not recognize the objective reality of your mental energies and their propensities for nonphysical travel, their influences remain hidden from you. Nevertheless, when you think of another person, energies corresponding to your energy patterns travel to that person, drawn by his or her mental space and energies. Likewise, every time anyone entertains a thought or feeling about you, corresponding energies travel from that person's mind to yours. Unless you are highly psychic, these communications register in mental regions that are part of your unconscious mind. However, as pointed out earlier, everything in the unconscious mind may be translated into the conscious arena.

So, if someone entertains a strong negative emotion regarding you, for example, it will register within your unconscious mental regions. Often it will be translated to the conscious arena, but with alterations. You may suddenly feel sad or angry, not knowing why. You may become irritable, or you may even think of the person who is thinking negatively about you and begin to feel negatively towards him or her. These reactions were stimulated by unconscious telepathic communications.

Not only occasional passing thoughts or emotions are transmitted to others. We constantly engage in telepathic communications. In the cases of individuals who are closely related, who have subjective proximity, the communications are more direct and more intense and therefore have greater effect. The emotional bonds between people who are closely related gives power to those inner communications. We have a vested interest psychically in those we know. Our successes and defeats, our happy moments and sad ones are telepathically transmitted to our friends and loved ones. We share in the experiences of those we know, and we continuously communicate our experiences to them.

Also, in subtle, usually unnoticed ways, our own mental energies are constantly affected and impressed by the mental energies of those with whom we are close. A mother will pick up on the illness of her distant child, before she would ever tune in to the illness of a stranger. Spouses find they are thinking the same thoughts. Lovers feel the presence of the loved one, no matter the distance separating them. Subjective mental proximity dramatically increases the intensity of telepathic communication: your thoughts will resonate more quickly with those of a friend; your emotions will be stirred sooner by the emotions of an enemy. Mental effects are increased through subjective proximity, but they are not limited to it.

Contributions to the Group Mind

As our physical actions may affect strangers, so do our mental actions and energies affect those we do not know. We have seen how the collective unconscious involves us all in an inner network of communication. We might consider this as what may be called a group mind. Here are stored the experiences, thoughts, and emotions of all those who have ever lived. Here we may find the record of the sufferings, joys, trials, and tribulations of every human being.

In your present state of consciousness, you may feel that your inner experiences, thoughts, and feelings are private and not available for anyone else to view. From the perspective of the conscious mind focused in physical reality, this is indeed the case. But deep within the mental dimensions, beyond all sense of separate ego, is a level where we share everything.

Our social concepts and social orders would not have evolved as far as they have if all communications had to take place one-on-one in the present moment. The thoughts of Aristotle, the realization of Buddha, the formulations of Pythagoras—these have all affected, and still affect, our social condition and mind far more than their historical placement would dictate. As Emerson said: "There is one mind common to all individual men. Every man is an inlet to the same and to all of the same. He that is once admitted to the right of reason is made a freeman of the whole estate. What Plato has thought, he may think; what a saint has felt, he may feel; what at any time has befallen any man, he can understand. Who hath access to this universal mind is a party to all that is or can be done, for this is the only and sovereign agent."[1]

Humanity is but one, though made up of many. Through the mental reservoir of the entire species, the unconscious portions of the indivdual mind have access to all that has gone before. Out of the unconscious regions of mind, each individual can learn to make conscious what he or she chooses. Only in this way have we been able effectively to build upon the realizations and events of the past.

Why is it that we frequently find the same scientific discovery made simultaneously at different points on the globe by different individuals? Why is it that a religious movement finds a place in the minds of thousands of individuals in the same period of history? Why do certain symbols mean the same thing to great masses of people without any conscious communication regarding them? It is because we all participate in the group mind.

From the storehouse of this group mind, each individual may choose what will be incorporated into his or her own awareness. According to the purposes, intentions, and desires of your conscious mind, your unconscious mental energies draw from the vast bank of human experiences. You may follow the same line of thinking as Descartes without even knowing who he was. An Aborigine may experience enlightenment with Gautama Buddha's help, without ever having heard of a Buddha.

It is also within the group mind that it is decided when humanity is ready for any new realization or discovery. Only when the collective weight of the group mind affirmed that we were ready for the discovery of nuclear energy, for example, was the discovery brought forth. When we are ready for a new discovery, various individuals will bring that discovery forth from the group mind, and from other regions of nonphysical reality, in order to manifest it physically. So, anyone may choose, according to their capacities and intentions, to serve to present humanity with the "gifts of the gods" by taking them out of the nonphysical dimensions in accordance with the dictates of the group mind.

The group mind is a kind of cosmic congress. Each thought you entertain that supports the concept of war is a vote for war in the group mind. Each time you feel faith in the overall goodness of all people, you place a vote of confidence in humanity. Your thoughts and feelings constitute your votes as to how you wish the course of humanity to proceed. And the majority rules.

The hidden effects of our mental energies are widespread. Not only do they affect those close to us through subjective proximity, and touch those far from us through the group mind; they also reach out to affect the world in which we live, as discussed in a later chapter. It will be helpful now to look at some of the ways in which we consciously use our mental energies to bring about effects in ourselves and in our experiences of the world.

CONSCIOUSLY CONTROLLED MENTAL ENERGIES

We often deliberately create mental structures and energy fields for the clear and concise purpose of bringing about some desired effect. In some cases we do so in an attempt to change ourselves. And at other times we create them with the obvious purpose of communicating our intentions beyond the confines of our private mental space. Even those who do not consciously believe in the transmission of mental energies at times act as though the phenomenon were real.

The principle behind conscious, purposive mental creations is essentially the same, no matter the form of creation we use or our intention. We create mental energy patterns and imbue them with direction, intention, and emotional energy. Once they are created and sent on their ways, we usually forget about them, trusting or hoping that they will go about their task of achieving the desired effect. We do this so often that we take the process for granted, as when we tell ourselves we must remember something later in the day and trust that the mental construct will return to remind us. But if we realized what we were doing, we could act more effectively and responsibly.

Self-suggestion

When you say to yourself, "Today I'm going to stand up to my boss," or, "I'm not going to give in to anger today," you're creating mental energy patterns for the purpose of bringing about changes within yourself. Quite consciously you are trying to implement new operational frameworks within your mind through self-suggestion.

"Positive thinking" is one of the newest forms of self-suggestion. It rests on the assumption that instilling positive attitudes about yourself or your world brings about changes in the way you act, feel, and perceive life. Assertiveness programs operate on the same principle.

Using such techniques you may, for example, tell yourself that you love yourself. In time, your mind will accept this suggestion as an operational framework, and you will come to feel better about yourself. Or, if you feel you are timid, you may regularly suggest to yourself that you are more forceful and aggressive. In either case you consciously implant new mental energies in the hope that they will change your psychological make-up, with the result of making your life better.

Self-suggestion generally requires repeated efforts. Your mental energy patterns were established over the course of time and are reinforced whenever you use them. Much energy has gone into the old patterns. In order to bring about effective changes, you must use enough mental energy to override the old patterns before the new ones can be allowed free play.

You give yourself suggestions constantly by means of your inner dialogue. You reinforce your beliefs and attitudes by mulling them over in your mind again and again. Usually you don't pay attention to this process. But when you take your own mental energies in hand and consciously attempt to implement new patterns of thinking and feeling, you are engaged in a process of conscious, self-controlled mental creation.

Desires

Not all the mental energy patterns we consciously create are intended to work solely within our private mental space. Desires are mental structures with high emotional charges. When you strongly desire something, you think about it often, and you imbue those thoughts with a strong force of attraction. To want something is to seek to draw it to yourself. Although you often act upon your desires physically, which is necessary for their realization, the mental energies of those desires are also acting within their own dimension.

Whether or not you are conscious of it, some portion of your mind knows the attractive properties of mental energies. Some aspect of your consciousness knows that your thoughts and emotions help shape your experiences of reality. Because of this you are inclined to dwell upon those things you desire in order to bring them into your life.

You may easily observe a nonphysical example of the highly attractive nature of desires. Watch your mind as you desire something. Your desire immediately attracts other thoughts and emotions relating to the original desire-energy. For example, if you desire money you automatically begin to visualize what you could do with that money. Associated fantasies come into the conscious mind. By simply thinking about what you desire, you can easily witness your mental energies attracting other patterns into your conscious mind. Repeatedly dwelling upon a desired object or event increases the desire-pattern's power.

The influences of desires affect our own mental patterns, but they range beyond our private mental space. When you desire something, you automatically transmit powerful telepathic signals out into the mental arena. You mentally communicate your desires to others, unconsciously hoping that they may be able to help you realize your desires. But your energies go even farther. Desires can affect physical reality. As discussed later, mental energies affect physical energies. This means that our mental energies have the potential of drawing events and objects into our lives. Under the right conditions, our desires are self-fulfilling.

The effectiveness of the energies of desires is determined by a number of different factors. The degree of energy is a critically important factor; the more you desire something the more mental energy you invest in it. Another factor is the clarity of the desire-signal: the more clear and precise your desire, the more effective it is. Also, mental energies working against your desire can interfere with its effectiveness. If for a long time you have believed that you will always be poor, then a desire for wealth will be inhibited and often overruled by that belief. And of course if your desire involves another person, their own purposes and intents enter into the outcome.

Desires are consciously formed mental energies that can go out into the world and achieve their ends. They are consciously controlled energies that range beyond the private mind. But as we all know, simply wishing for something does not make it happen. We have to take into consideration the overall patterns within our minds, in addition to our deep, inner purposes. We often desire something that would not be good for us. Remember the advice: "Be careful what you wish for; you may get it."

Prayer

Another obvious example of consciously created, mental energies that are intended to go beyond the private mental space is prayer. You do not pray to yourself. You are trying to communicate your feelings and thoughts to something beyond yourself. It may be asserted that God is present everywhere and our prayers need not go anywhere to be heard. But what about saints? A saint can hardly be listening to the thoughts of every human being, waiting to be called upon.

It very well may be that the greatest effect from prayers is on ourselves. By thinking about something higher, we raise the level of our thoughts, and at the very least stimulate higher aspects of our own consciousness. By directing our minds toward God, we increase the likelihood that our behavior will be more harmonious and moral. For most people the primary purpose for prayer is simply to send thoughts and feelings toward the Divine.

"Magic"

Throughout the centuries various individuals have been aware of the far-reaching effects of mental energies and used this knowledge to achieve desired ends. Consciously controlled mental creation associated with ritual, in accordance with the rules of a church, is called religion. Ritual used outside the church's framework is called magic.

It is not my intention to discuss the moral implications or value of magic. But it falls within the range of the current topic because it involves the conscious use of mental energies. Sometimes those involved in magic use physical objects in conjunction with the mind, for the purposes of mental focus and identification. Others work with the mind alone, as in the case of hermetic magic. There are those who believe that power lies not within the mind but with the objects or rituals, but these people are not conscious of what is going on at nonphysical levels.

Some magic is employed solely for transforming one's own consciousness; this is a kind of ritual for self-suggestion. In this practice people consciously address their own mental states and attempt to alter or transform them. Magic is also used to fulfill desires, or affect physical reality, or in some way alter the minds of others. All these uses involve the ritualistic creation of mental structures in order to employ mental power.

Although the term "magic" has a negative connotation to many, everyone uses the technique, either consciously or unconsciously. For example, the simple process of repeating something over and over to memorize it involves a repetitive ritualistic control of mental energies. As our understanding of the mind and its powers increases, the mystery will be lessened and magic as something unnatural will become an archaic concept replaced by a true science of the mind. Only mystery and ritual separate magic from desire; once we evolve beyond the need for these, "magic" will be an obsolete concept.

Conscious Extrasensory Perception

We have already seen how telepathic communications occur at an unconscious level. There are some individuals, however, who are able to employ this method of communication consciously. Some do so intentionally, and others do so spontaneously. Extrasensory perception initiated intentionally involves consciously controlled mental energies.

When we attempt to send telepathic messages, first we create either a mental image or a pattern containing information. Then we attempt to send the image or message to the mind of another. Clarity, power, and personal translations influence our effectiveness.

As we can send mental energies and patterns, we can also seek them out. You can direct your mind to seek out information telepathically by creating a mental pattern to attract the information sought. This "seeker-form" is then sent through the mental dimension in quest of the desired information. Psychics occasionally use this method when attempting to locate a missing person.

In clairvoyance the issue is a little different. Instead of mind-to-mind communication, one attempts to sense the vibrational energies of an object. The clairvoyant then attempts to match the energies with a similar pattern stored in the memory. A sensitive would never be able to identify a totally unfamiliar object.

Telepathy, clairvoyance, and similar phenomena are but a few more examples of the ways in which we can and do consciously create mental energy fields. In each case mental patterns are created, sought, or received via the mental dimension. There are no doubt many other available applications of this procedure, applications which may be discovered through an exploration of one's own mindscape.

The effectiveness of any attempt to achieve some desired end through the conscious creation of mental patterns and energies depends strongly upon the nature of the individual's personal mental space and matrix. I have hinted at some of the ways in which the structure of one's mind may affect such things as self-suggestion, desire, and telepathy. A deeper understanding of the nature of belief systems is now in order. In the next chapter I consider the personal mental matrix and the ways it governs one's relationship with oneself and with reality.

6

The Private Mental Matrix

To know with absolute certainty is not given to us. Even the most solid of scientific "facts" may be overthrown by new discoveries. The reliability of our perceptions of the world may be questioned, as becomes apparent as various people perceive the same event in very different ways. Since we do not perceive directly but via the physical senses, which may be affected by any number of subjective factors, we cannot say that the senses give us a perfectly objective description of reality. Each of us is unique, and the way we see the world is equally unique.

Fortunately there is enough agreement about the arrangement of the physical world for us to relate coherently to one another. Though we may not agree on how the world was formed or its ultimate nature, for the most part we can agree on its appearance. But there is far more involved in our perceptions of the nature of reality than the appearance of the physical world. Politics, religion, social issues, ethical issues, philosophical speculations—these and many other topics raise highly subjective questions. We all have opinions, and we all have personal beliefs that color and influence our perceptions.

We choose our own beliefs, sometimes unconsciously, but usually as the result of conscious decisions. Personal observations and judgments combine in the process of forming beliefs, but other factors are involved as well. Sometimes our beliefs are determined by the way we wish things were. Reasoning and emotion mix and merge to affect what we believe. Other people influence our beliefs. Sometimes they arise as the result of irrational assumptions.

Whatever the reasons we adopt a belief or a set of beliefs, they implant an operational framework of mental energies within the mind. Every belief is stored as a guideline according to which you relate to all of reality. Everything you do results from the belief patterns in your mind, and your reactions to events or situations are determined by your beliefs and their accompanying emotional energies. Everything you feel or think about yourself is determined by your beliefs.

We all believe differently; no two people believe exactly the same things. Could this mean that only your beliefs are correct? Or does it mean that we are all limited in our understanding of the nature of reality, and that we all harbor some false beliefs? I believe that is the case.

It is all too common for people to adopt a set of beliefs and then tenaciously cling to them. We tend to identify with our beliefs, and when someone challenges them we take it as a personal attack. Heated arguments ensue, rarely with the result of any change of views. Sometimes people kill or are killed for their beliefs. Conflicting beliefs have led to wars and persecutions. Narrow beliefs have held back understanding throughout the ages.

To grow and to evolve requires that we learn new things and adopt new ways of viewing reality. Growth requires willingness to accept the possibility that our present beliefs might be limited or inaccurate. It requires willingness to implement new beliefs. But none of this is possible unless you examine what it is you believe.

INTERPLAY OF BELIEFS WITHIN PRIVATE MENTAL SPACE

We all have inner conflicts. Regardless of our relationships with external reality, we must first face and live with ourselves. No matter how pleasant our life situation, we must contend with our own thoughts and emotions, and these often give us trouble.

In this day and age it seems that psychological problems are all too abundant. People suffer from depression and anxiety. They are neurotic or schizophrenic. They have feelings of inadequacy and irrational fears. There are countless mental patterns that upset the balance and harmony of the private mental space.

We cannot blame our inner conflicts on the world around us. We may say that if things were different, if people would change, everything would be all right within us, but this is not so. Ultimately we are totally responsible for our own inner state. No matter the outer conditions, if you are not at peace with yourself and happy in your existence, it is because of mental patterns you have created that interact with each other in such a way as to prevent your peace and happiness.

Field Interactions in the Private Belief Matrix

We have already touched briefly on the nature of beliefs as operational guidelines within the mind. Not only do beliefs govern all ingoing and outgoing perceptions and actions, but all internal activity also depends on your operational system. Your feelings are largely determined by the way you believe you *should* feel in any given situation. Your thoughts come and go as a result of and according to the nature of the mental patterns comprising your beliefs. As we have seen, much of this takes place on an unconscious level.

Consider your dilemma if you had two bosses and at the same time each of them ordered you to do something right away. You would be in a no-win situation. The same sort of situation frequently occurs within the mind. For example, imagine that you are poor. Further, you believe that poor people are relatively worthless. Still, you believe that you are a worthwhile person. You would be harboring contradictory beliefs, inevitably resulting in mixed feelings about yourself.

Consider another example. Imagine that you want to explore the hidden recesses of your own vast mental space. Imagine also that you believe the deeper portions of the mind are filled with chaotic and oftentimes frightening impulses. On the one hand, you want to explore your own nature, but on the other hand, you believe that you have reason to fear what you might find. Inner conflict ensues.

Contradictory or opposing energy patterns and beliefs create incompatible energy fields within the mind. They are like the positive poles of two magnets pushing against each other. If the opposing beliefs or mental structures are important enough to you, then you experience constant inner tension.

The mind does not choose by itself which beliefs to operate from. In a given situation, every belief that applies is activated, and the mind indicates the actions that would follow each belief. You, the self, must consciously deal with the discrepancies and contradictions.

Your beliefs about yourself primarily determine your

moment-to-moment state of mind and emotion. It is not easy to become aware of what you believe about yourself. But it is necessary if you are ever to have strong, positive feelings about yourself and the world. If as a child you became firmly convinced that you could do nothing right, as an adult you may never feel right about anything you do. If you believe that at heart you are sinful, you will always hold yourself suspect. Or, perhaps more critically, if you believe you are powerless to bring about changes within yourself, you will never achieve greater self-realization and self-fulfillment.

It is not my intention to tell you what you should believe. I only wish to point out that your beliefs establish operational energy patterns within your mind, and these determine the way you see yourself and the world. If you have mutually exclusive or contradictory energy patterns, you will experience inner conflict. If you have rigid energy patterns, your thinking will be inflexible and you will prevent yourself from conceiving of new ways of seeing things. If you have self-undermining mental patterns, then you will travel a downhill course toward depression and impotence.

Of course, the energy matrix of your belief system operates in positive ways as well. Sets of beliefs that complement and strengthen each other yield an effective operational framework. Belief systems that allow for change and growth serve to increase your potentials. Recognizing the limitations of your own awareness keeps you from being bound to any one belief or belief system.

Beliefs you have about yourself determine the way you relate to yourself. You may decide in the morning that you are going to feel good about yourself that day, but if you have had poor faith in yourself for many years you will automatically override the short-term suggestion. The mind retains and operates by existing belief patterns unless the necessary energy is applied to bring about substantial inner changes.

It is easier to examine your beliefs about politics, social issues, or other people than to examine your beliefs about yourself. You cannot help but examine your beliefs through the filter of those very beliefs. But as mentioned before, beliefs also generate the constant flow of thoughts. Therefore, if you pay attention to your thoughts and feelings throughout the day, your beliefs will become apparent. Conflicting conscious thoughts reveal the presence and the nature of conflicting inner energy fields. For this reason, we may be thankful for the conflicts within our daily thought-patterns: they provide us with keys to and opportunities for self-improvement.

Priority Levels Within the Private Belief Matrix

Within the mental matrix there are varying priorities of belief. Those that are critical to one's sense of self and to one's balance within the current system of reality hold top priority. They will brook no change without a corresponding change in one's sense of self. They are not easily addressed, nor are they easily changed.

Slightly lower on the priority scale are those beliefs that pertain to one's perspective on the nature of reality. These, too, can be hard to change simply because they are so seldom questioned. They may involve such things as belief in God, questions regarding purpose in life, issues of good and evil, or of free will versus determinism.

On another level one may encounter belief structures concerned with life's myriad experiences. Political, religious, social, and psychological attitudes are most often found at this level. Many of these beliefs do change over the course of time as experience is gained and other viewpoints are encountered. They may be investigated and addressed fairly easily.

Finally, there are superficial beliefs that may change from day to day, more properly called attitudes or opinions. It often takes little more than a change of mood to alter one's opinion on a passing topic. These attitudes and opinions, though capable of playing a significant role in determining how we relate to the reality we encounter, are very unstable and may easily be overruled by deeper belief patterns.

This gradation of beliefs involves not only the relative permanence of each belief; it also involves operational priorities. Easily changed, relatively superficial beliefs may be effectively thwarted by more deep-seated beliefs. The conscious belief or attitude you hold in the passing moment will not take precedence over long-standing beliefs. Revelations leading to inspiration and new, positive attitudes will gradually lose their power if a belief of higher priority is in conflict with them. This is why often we cannot hold on to those moments of high inspiration and revelation; we retain mental energy fields with enough power to drain the new concept of its effectiveness.

Long-held and emotionally charged beliefs are stronger than new beliefs and stronger than those of a strictly intellectual nature. Beliefs that are more comprehensive in their operational nature have more effect than those that apply to particulars or isolated situations.

Many of our deepest beliefs, which hold an almost unchallenged position of high priority, were adopted when we were quite young. Some of these were tele-pathically communicated to us as infants. For example, few of us question that we are separate from our environment and from other people. This is a cultural belief that was instilled in our minds before we ever learned to speak. It affects how we perceive all of reality and how we think of ourselves. But is it true, or is it unnecessarily limiting?

We also have beliefs about ourselves and reality that were adopted in accordance with our early religious teachings. These, when placed next to newer beliefs and hopes, often lead to priority conflicts. Can we trust our own impulses, for example, if we became thoroughly convinced at an early age that we are sinful? Many people suffer from personal guilt that originated in religious teachings that permeate our society. Where did you get your first conceptions of God? Do those conceptions conflict with newer, broader perspectives?

These deeper beliefs may seem too philosophical to apply to our everyday concerns, but on closer examination it will be seen that they directly affect everything in our lives. Our first beliefs regarding the nature of good and evil, if unchanged, still govern our values and methods for achieving our desired goals. A belief that the individual is separate from all else strongly affects how we behave towards others and towards our environment. A belief that human nature is inherently sinful clouds every feeling we may have about ourselves and challenges and often overrides any attempts to instill personal feelings of grace and self-worth.

As we mature we naturally attempt to improve our system of beliefs. Too often, however, we do this by trying to force new beliefs into our minds without removing the old ones. Which take priority? Old beliefs do not go away by themselves. Being composed of highly charged mental structures, they remain within our minds and carry out their purpose, unless we put forth the effort necessary to disassemble them. This generally requires closely examining them and, if necessary, convincing ourselves they are unsound.

Sometimes a belief system may be overhauled quickly, as in the case of a religious conversion taking place in a time of crisis. Sometimes a belief system may contain so many contradictions and self-defeating precepts that a great inner crisis builds within the individual. Inner conflicts may so overwhelm a person that he or she loses functional effectiveness and, as a result of the confusion, can no longer deal with reality. When such a crisis is reached, an individual may be forced to undergo rapid and radical change.

These radical changes may be positive or negative. Mental and emotional breakdowns may ensue. Acts of despair or temporary insanity could develop. Or, a whole new set of beliefs may be adopted with little consideration of their value, and the old set summarily dismissed. On the positive side, a beneficial revamping of self-image may quickly develop when a crisis leads one to discover previously unrecognized reservoirs of inner strength. Such a rapid change may or may not be permanent.

Such crises occur only after individuals have not taken stock of their beliefs for some time. Periodic re-evaluation of your beliefs and attitudes regarding yourself and reality allows for gradual and harmonious changes to take place. But if conflicting beliefs are allowed to increase in power for too long, then the whole mental structure may give way under the stress. It is like trying to build a house without taking note of structural strengths and architectural design. The house may stand for a long time, but as more and more weight is added to it, the stresses increase until the whole structure falls to the ground.

We must recognize the priority levels within our belief systems. We have to explore our own mental patterns deeply so that we may become aware of the foundation beliefs upon which so many other beliefs stand. We have to know the whole range of our mental structures in order to know what fits into them harmoniously and what only increases inner conflicts.

You have determined the various levels of priority within your belief structure. You have delegated the power to each belief, each attitude. And you still have the power to make any changes you deem necessary.

We hold even deeper beliefs that are rarely examined. For example, most of us believe unquestionably that we are forced to adhere to the laws of physical reality. We firmly believe that the ground upon which we stand will continue to support us, as dictated by physical laws. We believe that we cannot fly under our own power without some machine. We believe that we cannot travel through time. Is it possible that even these beliefs may be questioned? Could it be that we are not as limited in what we can do and perceive as these beliefs indicate?

INTERPLAY OF THE BELIEF MATRIX WITH EXTERNAL REALITY

The mental energy patterns comprising your private belief matrix influence not only your relationship with yourself; they also determine your relationships with the world you perceive. As the operational framework of the mind, the belief matrix dictates the pattern of actions and reactions you manifest in the world. You draw upon your past experiences and feelings about them in order to determine how you will function or act in any particular situation. You also perceive your reality through the filter of your beliefs. So, the effects of your belief system in regard to external reality manifest through a two-way process: you perceive through them and you act through them. Let's investigate these one at a time.

The Perception of Reality through the Belief Matrix

Beliefs do not play such an important part in our perceptions of purely physical reality. What we perceive from our narrow focus within the physical realm is determined by much deeper beliefs and mental matrices. But our conscious beliefs play a strong part in the realm of our relationships to that which we perceive. How we feel about what we perceive, what we think about that which is before us, how we behave toward all we encounter, these are strongly determined by energy patterns which serve as our operational frameworks.

When you perceive or encounter something, your first action is unconscious. It involves mentally registering the information detected by your physical senses. Secondly, you refer this information to your belief matrix. You may do this consciously or without thinking about the process. In either case the process usually occurs in something like the following fashion. You see a man approaching you on the sidewalk. You ask yourself what you should think and feel as a result of seeing him. Your beliefs may tell you that by assessing his outward appearance you may gain more information to aid you in your judgment. So you look at him more closely, perhaps making note of his clothing, his posture, the expression on his face, and the color of his skin. With this information in mind, you refer to your beliefs again. What do you believe about a person that wears a suit, or one that is dressed in tattered, disordered clothing? What do you believe about someone who has a straight posture, or one who stoops over when walking? What do you believe about someone who has squinting eyes or a tight-lipped expression? And what do you believe about someone whose skin is white or black or red?

All of these considerations and referrals to the standing belief patterns take place quickly, usually automatically. Combining what you physically perceive with what you believe about what you perceive, you will likely make some quick decision about this man approaching you. If you believe that you are encountering a potentially hostile individual, you will tense up in preparation for the possibility of a dangerous encounter. If you believe that you are facing a trustworthy individual, you might smile or say hello.

This process of perception, referral to the belief network, and judgment takes place constantly. It is only because we do not pay attention and because the process takes place so rapidly that we do not realize what is going on. Reactions to remarks about ourselves are another example of this process. When someone says something about you which you do not like, you may react with anger. This results from beliefs established over the course of time. You interpret the remark as an insult, in some way damaging to your self-image. Or you may believe that your reputation will be harmed by it. Your reasons for reacting to a situation with anger are based upon your resident beliefs.

What do you believe about our relation to nature and the environment? If you believe that all natural resources exist only to serve the needs of humanity, your actions toward the environment will be dictated by this belief. In such a case you ignore the needs of other creatures and the ecological ramifications of exploiting natural resources. You likely never even entertain the possibility that trees and animals are conscious beings with rights.

Your perceptions of other human beings are dictated by your beliefs as well. Do you have blanket beliefs about all those who belong to races other than your own? If so, you perceive all people of other races through the filter of that belief, not allowing yourself to see the true individual differences among all people. If you have negative prejudices, they will prevent you from seeing the positive attributes of others.

People tend to take their beliefs about reality as facts. Whether from a belief in our infallibility or from lazy mental habits, we too often form opinions and beliefs and then operate as if they reflected the absolute truth about the nature of reality. But whenever we operate from any limited belief system, there is ample opportunity for errors of judgment and perception. As Charles T. Tart has said: "At one level, each human being, functioning in his ordinary d-SoC (discrete state of consciousness) . . . shows selective perception, selective thinking, selective action that in turn controls his perceptions. Because of his particular culture and the consensus reality to which his ordinary d-SoC has adapted him, plus his personal idiosyncrasies, he (1) is more prone to observe certain things; (2) is unlikely to observe other kinds of things at all; and (3) may have a great many transformations and distortions of what he does sense before it reaches his consciousness. This all happens unconsciously, automatically, and smoothly in the normally functioning adult." [1]

As said before, your mind does not generally make value judgments about the relative worth of your beliefs. It obediently registers the energies you set up and then proceeds to use these as its operational parameters. It is conceivable for an individual to retain nothing but false beliefs about the nature of reality and about himself or herself. In such a case the mind continues to operate just as if all those beliefs were true.

Since our mental energies are transmitted telepathically to others, our false beliefs reinforce the same energy patterns within others who believe the same way. Individuals with negative prejudices reinforce such negative beliefs in others, whether they are verbally communicated or not. Our beliefs about the nature of reality have widespread effects.

The mind is an amazing thing. If you believe strongly that things are a certain way, then you may not be able to see evidence which contradicts this belief, even when it appears right before your eyes. If, for example, you believe another person is totally selfish, you will interpret any selfless act they perform as arising from selfish motives, as a devious form of selfishness. Thus it will appear to you that what you perceive reinforces your original belief in his or her selfishness.

Similarly, if you do not believe in telepathy, you will never knowingly experience it. Thoughts originating in the mind of another may come into your mind, or you and another person may think the same thing at the same time. But you would never recognize this for what it is because of your belief pattern.

The matrix of energies that constitute your belief system form a web of forces that exclude all perceptions and information not meshing with that web. Anything you perceive which does not accord with the already existing patterns of energy within your mind will be either reshaped to fit or excluded altogether from your conscious awareness. Nothing is ever forced into your mind, whether it is true or false. The matrix of energies you have built determines what comes in and what goes out.

Imagine that you always wear a pair of glasses with red lenses. You would never see greens. The same would happen if you believe that there are no greens in the world: you would be unable to perceive or recognize the color green. It is not difficult to deceive oneself.

Consider those burdened with extreme paranoia. They believe that everyone is out to get them and perceive hostility in everyone they meet. They cannot see that no one really has it in for them. Their beliefs dictate their picture of the world. Accordingly, they avoid others and live in fear.

The paranoid person is an extreme example and one that is easily recognized since the symptoms are so obvious. But to a lesser degree the same principle occurs with all of us. We all have some false beliefs, and these give us a partially false picture of the world. On the basis of this partially false picture, we determine how to behave towards others and towards our environment.

Action and Creation through the Belief Matrix

We have already seen a few ways in which our actions are determined by our beliefs, but there are more. Our capacities and limitations are greatly influenced by what we believe, by our personal attitudes. Our abilities, potentials, and effectiveness are all affected by mental energy patterns.

Take individuals who are convinced that they are incapable of comprehending some subject. Their conviction is self-fulfilling. They will probably never make an attempt to study that subject. If they do, they will be so convinced that it is beyond them that they will not allow comprehension to take place.

The same thing often happens with powers of creativity. Everyone has immense potentials for creativity. Many people, however, repeatedly tell themselves that they could never learn to play music, or that painting is beyond them, or that they do not have the literary intelligence needed to write. Such things are true only if we believe they are true. We are fully capable of limiting ourselves by beliefs that have restrictive mental energies. Students who believe that they are stupid may be unable to learn. People facing a new and unexpected handicap may believe that they cannot overcome it, and they don't. These are examples of people unnecessarily limiting themselves by adopting limiting beliefs. Whether such beliefs come from others or we create them, we make them come true by adhering to them.

It is just as easy, if not easier, to adopt and reinforce positive mental energy patterns. You can believe in your creative abilities, in your own worth, in your intelligence and ability to learn, and these can become just as self-fulfilling as negative beliefs. Take, for example, two children with the same inherent abilities. Constantly tell one that he will never accomplish anything. Simultaneously tell the other that she can do anything she sets her mind to. Which child will accomplish more in life?

People often complain about their situation in life and maintain that they can do nothing about it. This betrays a belief in powerlessness. Their belief system is the only thing preventing such people from making changes in their life situations. That can be a powerful obstacle.

We tend to think that our beliefs result from our experiences. We think that we believe the way we do because we have seen evidence to support those beliefs. But in truth the process works in the reverse order. First come the beliefs, then perception of reality in accordance with those beliefs. This gives the appearance that reality is confirming our beliefs. So we cling ever more tenaciously to them, proclaiming that we can see evidence in support of them everywhere. This point cannot be emphasized too strongly: You do not believe as you believe because of your perceptions of reality. You perceive reality the way you do because of your beliefs.

Again and again we must turn inward to find the key to our experiences of reality. We ourselves are the key. Our minds are the tool with which we shape our perceptions and attract our experiences. So long as we believe the power is in the external world, we are indeed powerless to effect change. But once we accept the power that is rightfully ours, all things are possible.

SUBJECTIVE MEMORY

At times memory is a function of belief. You will recall experiences you value or invest with strong emotional energy more clearly than other experiences. You impress your mind with an experience to the degree that you believe it is worth remembering. According to your beliefs, you determine what and how you remember.

We have all had the experience in school of believing that the material we study has no value. As students, we might believe that we will never need to know the succession of the kings of England, and so we impress our minds with the information just enough to remember it for the test. A few months later the knowledge is gone.

Even if we do not value an experience, it is still impressed upon the mind. To one degree or another all experiences are registered within the mind's energy fields. As time passes, value judgments dictate which can be recalled. If we had particularly unpleasant experiences in childhood, we can block our memory of them from all conscious awareness. On the other hand, if we need to recall the name of someone we have not thought of for some time, with a bit of effort we can usually do so. We partially determine what we can recall from the past by what we believe is important.

Even with recently experienced events, memory is affected by belief. It is common for different people to recall the same event in different ways. Although they saw exactly the same thing, they emphasize different elements. Because of differing beliefs they may have actually perceived the event in different ways. For example, two people see a fight between a white man and a black man; one prejudiced against white people will more likely recall that the white man started the fray, whether it occurred that way or not.

Our psychological impressions of things and events also color our memories. We may choose to remember a little clump of trees where we played as a child as an immense forest. Even though we had a poverty-stricken, deprived childhood, we may recall that period of our lives as one of the most pleasant. No matter how poor we were, if we so choose we can remember the days of our poverty as days of wealth. We are equally capable of blocking negative memories to the extent that for us the experiences behind them never occurred.

All of these situations involve current beliefs effectively influencing our pictures of the past. We have stored, sorted, and implanted memories according to our beliefs about how the experiences unfolded, and according to the values we place on those experiences. Not only does our memory play tricks on us: we also play tricks on our memory.

BELIEF AND THE RELATIVITY OF REALITY

Each of us has a unique perspective on the world. As a result of our beliefs, we all see the world differently and according to different guidelines. Einstein's Theory of Relativity demonstrates that the perception of time and space depends upon the position of the observer. In our overall picture of reality, our perception of experiences is dependent upon our internal position—our beliefs.

For all practical purposes we each see an entirely different world. The mental currents, polarities, and patterns residing within each mind construct widely varying viewpoints. Attitudes, philosophies, religions, political views—these are but a few of the aspects of our beliefs that color our perceptions. What we consider to be good or evil casts shadows over everything; the way we believe things should be affects what we see and how we judge what we see.

The nature of objective reality aside from our perception of it is not really the important issue. Objective facts do not lead to wars; it is subjective perceptions and beliefs about the facts that lead to wars. Moral actions do not stem from objective reality; they stem from subjective reality. Differences of opinion do not arise from differences in the objective world; they arise from differences in the ways we each see the world.

Every perspective may be somewhat valid within its own frame of reference. The point is not to find out who is right and who is wrong. The point is that we are unique individuals, and we must necessarily perceive the world from our own perspective. But we must remember that it is a perspective, and that it does not necessarily mirror reality perfectly. All perspectives are limited, and in the final analysis no perspective is the right one.

Through the interchange of beliefs we can gain wider visions and clearer perspectives. We must be willing to recognize our own limitations if we are ever to transcend them. So long as we hold our beliefs about reality to be facts about reality, we lock ourselves into a limited viewpoint. The patterns of energy that are within our minds must continually change if growth is to occur. Perspectives on reality are relative to the observer, and if any perspective is more true than any other, it must be the perspective that takes all others into consideration and recognizes their value.

Part 3

Part 3

7

Translating Mental Reality into Physical Reality

Until now I have been discussing primarily the nature of the constructions and patterns that exist and operate within the mind. But how does the objective reality of mental creations bear upon our lives, aside from the obvious psychological ways? To what degree do our mental patterns and fluctuations influence the nature of our relationship with reality? Hopefully, the ensuing material will shed some light on these questions.

There is mounting evidence that physical reality has nonphysical underpinnings. Recent findings in the field of quantum physics give striking support to the proposition that reality is multidimensional, and that much of the mechanism of reality operates at energy levels outside the range of physical reality's parameters. I go into the specifics of these findings later. For now it is enough to bear in mind that evidence indicates that physical reality continuously rises from and is supported by vast resources of energy that exist in other dimensions.

It is reasonable to believe that these other-dimensional energies require a guiding force in order to take physical form. I hope to demonstrate that this force is consciousness and mind. I believe that we, and all other forms of consciousness, guide, shape, and direct the multidimensional energies of creation into those shapes and events we choose to see made manifest, whether we do so consciously or unconsciously. We are all cocreators, and reality is our project. Much of the process of creation is enacted from the sphere of the higher Self, but much is also accomplished by the actions of the private self we perceive ourselves as being.

It might be easier to understand how we translate mental energies into physical energies if we understand how the process involves us personally. To that end let's look at the way we set into motion those forces that shape our private perceptions and experiences of life and reality. From there we can proceed to an investigation of the ways in which we work together to form our shared reality.

MENTAL EVENTS

Nothing is truly static. Everything is part of the dance of energy and consciousness. Therefore, all things may be seen as events. A rock is an event, as are all objects. They do not just sit lifelessly but constantly emerge into existence from the deeper dimensions of reality. Even without considering the nonphysical aspects of reality, we can see that the most inert of objects has hidden within it the play of atoms, electrons, and quanta. Events are not only things that obviously change over the course of time like action scenarios; all things are events. Each thought is a mental event, as is each daydream. All things involve not only the state of being, but the state of becoming. You and I are events. We are more than beings; we are ever-changing, multidimensional events in the domain of reality. So now let's delve into the nature of mental events.

The Formation of Mental Events

We are all familiar with basic mental events—we perceive them in our daydreams and in our imaginings. Very often we encounter them quite directly in those dreams which are mentally-formed scenarios. We perceive mental scenarios as extended events just as we perceive physical scenarios; they involve a series of images and impressions evolving over the course of time.

Our minds, under the stimulation of our wills and intentions, create these events in the nonphysical dimensions quite easily. We have only to make the barest of efforts to initiate the most fantastic mental dramas. We can envision ourselves in a splendid palace or evoke the image of a distant loved one. At times a sequence of events or scenarios will pass before our mental vision spontaneously, seemingly without any effort on our part. Our dreams especially seem to unfold effortlessly.

These mental events are formed of mental energies. Various patterns and structures are reproduced, interwoven, and developed. We draw upon the storehouse of our experiential memories with lightning speed as, for example, we see ourselves and a loved one along with images of trees and lakes and weave them together into a delightful, romantic scene. Or we summon our acquired and developed philosophical systems before our mental vision, so that we can interject new elements and extract new realizations. We can create any number of mental events almost instantaneously.

If we had to reproduce all of our mental images and

events in physical form, the task would be so time-consuming that we would soon despair. But in the mindscape, creation of a highly complex order is quite natural. In the mind we are as gods, able to unfurl the pageantry of worlds and civilizations, drawing from the ethereal energy of nonphysical realms to create new life and order. What we imagine, is. What we intend becomes as we intend it, without even a wave of the hand.

Truly, in the realm of the mind, we have the powers that we have traditionally ascribed to the gods. But to what ends do we use these powers? Obviously we sometimes simply choose to amuse ourselves. Yet much of the time there is a more constructive purpose behind our mental activities. Our main field of interest lies within the physical realm; a primary focus of our consciousness is here. It is in this, the physical dimension, that we are most concerned with seeing our creations come to life and fruition. Our mental activities are often concerned with our efforts at physical creation.

Mental Events and Physical Reality

There are a variety of ways in which our mental events impinge upon our experiences in physical reality. Our self-created dreams often involve the reconstruction of waking events; we created them for the purpose of reviewing, assessing, and evaluating our physical actions and experiences. We seem to have a need to re-create our experiences and look at them from every side. We need to approach them from different directions and experiment with different ways of enacting them. From all these mental evaluations we make in dreams, we may awaken with the intention of putting our newly gained perspectives to work in creating a more fulfilling life.

We perform the same mental operations while we are awake. Especially just prior to taking some action or making some decision, we create mental events pertaining to the issue at hand, and we juggle the possibilities. How many times does a man mentally propose marriage before he ever takes physical action? In choosing a new house, don't people mentally place themselves in each one under consideration in an effort to see which they like best and feel most comfortable in?

We use mental events to reflect upon and learn from experiences we encounter in physical reality. We also use them to help us choose from various possible courses of action. In this latter case they serve as mock situations allowing us tentatively to choose a path of action, see how it feels, and then turn back and try again if we don't like the way it seems to go. But there are even more direct relationships between some of our mental actions or scenarios, and our physical experiences.

Once we decide how we want things to progress in our lives, we don't just let the issue drop, especially if it involves some uncertainty about how to proceed. Suppose that your current, fondest desire is to own your own home, but you do not at present have the means to realize it. You will do what you can physically to hasten the realization of that goal, and you will probably think about it frequently. You might mentally picture the type of house you want and place it in the desired setting. As the days and weeks progress, you may imagine yourself in that home, and picture the type of neighbors that you wish to have. Over the course of time, you construct an intricate picture of your goal and you dwell on it from time to time, all the while filling this mental image with emotional energies.

Such mental activity affects your motivation. It is easier, for example, to stay at a disagreeable job if it helps you realize some goal. In addition you are creating a mental blueprint with shape, structure, energy and direction. It is the psychic blueprint for what you wish to see manifested. This occurs with any desire you repeatedly envision.

This blueprint differs from physical blueprints in one important way; it is not simply a pattern from which to work but in fact the structural heart of a physical event. The energies that compose mental events, when imbued with the proper images, forces, and intentions, actually serve as an energy field around which physical reality begins to form. The mental event and structure are a pattern and an attractive field initiating the process of physical materialization. In this way the "power of the gods" which we have in our minds is brought forth into the physical dimension; in this way we strive to manifest those creative powers and abilities that are normally the province of the higher, less limited Self.

THE FORMATION OF PHYSICAL EVENTS

I have said that there are no closed systems. The physical dimension is not isolated from the nonphysical realm; by necessity they interact and interweave. We arbitrarily draw a line that separates them. We make the division according to our physical senses: what we can perceive physically, we label as being of the domain of physical reality. The rest is considered as either unreal or as existing in another dimension. But as we shall see when we look into physics, on close examination we find that the line of division does not exist at all.

It is not my intention here to elaborate on all the points at which various dimensions touch. I just want to make you aware that the mind plays an important part in the translation of energies between dimensions. Also, it is central to the shaping and attracting of physical experiences and events.

Translating Mental Energies into Physical Energies

Consciousness lies at the heart of all things. Behind the smallest packet of humanly detectable energy there is consciousness. And all consciousness has the impetus toward self-expression. There is no fixed form or predetermined channel for this self-expression. Predetermined form implies the presence of external restraints, but there are none. Consciousness is multidimensional, and its expressions are multidimensional.

Self-expression is always a cooperative process. Nothing exists in a vacuum; it is clear that all things are interdependent and interrelated. We could not express ourselves verbally without a shared language. We could not express ourselves physically without the cooperation of atoms and molecules and other physical factors. We all participate in a finely interwoven process of cooperation.

The energy that composes our physical bodies does not belong to us. The cells and atoms have a life of their own, even though for a time they participate in the formation of these bodies. As Annie Besant said, "Every cell in the body is composed of myriads of tiny lives, each with its own germinal consciousness." [1] So when we pass from our bodies, the cells and atoms carry on, taking on new forms and participating in new creations. The energy within our minds also has its own independent validity. Fortunately, its manner of expression coincides with our needs.

At times we choose to work for or with others in a group or institution. But we still retain our independent existence and validity. Every aspect of consciousness operates on the same principle. Being part of one cooperative process, being in fact part of one continuous whole, the individual aspects work together in an ultimately common cause, even while retaining their independent inviolability. Once again from Annie Besant, "We cannot too often remind ourselves that consciousness is one; that all apparently separate consciousnesses are truly one, as one sea might pour through many holes in an embankment." [2]

It is in line with the purposes and intents of certain nonphysical energies and the consciousness that lies at their heart to participate in the formation of mental structures, patterns, and gestalts. Aligning themselves with a mind such as yours or mine affords these energies greater opportunities for expression. And greater opportunities for expression are likewise afforded us through participating with them.

Now, as our physical bodies are partial expressions of our inner natures, so may physical manifestation serve as a partial expression for nonphysical energies and gestalts of consciousness. As said before, we, with our minds, have the power of giving shape and new form to mental energies: as we create a mental event it becomes real in the nonphysical dimension. The free-ranging energies which may coalesce to give body to such creations have their own consciousness. They come together in accordance with our design because it suits their purposes to participate in our creations. So, the thoughts or mental events we shape have lives of their own.

In some cases, we hope to see the mental event become a physical event. We wish to see the objects of our desires made manifest physically. In essence we are seeking and intending to extend an expression of our mental events into the realm of physical events. This accords with the intents of the energies that compose our mental events, since they have the impetus to express themselves in as many ways and on as many levels of reality as possible. In simple terms, they too would like to be born into physical reality.

We have then a structure composed of mental energies imbued with not only our desire for it to come to physical manifestation, but also the impetus toward further manifestation that is inherent in consciousness. This structure of energy and expression of consciousness may be seen as a living blueprint with the urge toward physical materialization. It stands at the threshold of physical reality.

At present we do not know what the mechanism is on the physical side of the process. It may involve infinitesimally small packets of energy, or quanta, which we may assume like other energies seek further expression. They, too, participate in cooperative events. They interact at the level of subatomic particles that cluster to form atoms and so on, until full-fledged physical objects and events occur. These quanta stand at the threshold of nonphysical reality. This will become clearer when we get into quantum physics. They stand so close to the threshold that they may be affected by and communicate with nonphysical energies.

Perhaps at the subsubatomic level, physical energy is impressed by the intents and patterns of nonphysical energies. Is it possible that the physical world can hear and respond to our mental and emotional energies? This does not imply that we can think of a diamond and eventually one will pop into existence out of thin air, although there is some evidence among Eastern gurus that this is possible. If we continually imagine a diamond in our hand, it would more likely become a reality through someone giving us a diamond, though the mechanism may be unclear.

So we have mental or nonphysical energies shaping a structure in accordance with a purpose and design, and this may be communicated to physical energies. The mental event is now on its way to becoming a physical event. If this occurs, the consciousness that was inherent within the mental event may focus itself in the physical event. Consciousness is independent of the parameters of any dimension. It would seem that, just as we temporarily focus our consciousness in and around our physical bodies, so can other aspects of consciousness focus in and around physical events and objects. But in each case consciousness requires a vehicle that corresponds to each dimension in which it seeks to express itself and participate.

Physical Events and Private Mental Energies

From the individual's standpoint, this process of the transference of mental patterns and intents into the physical domain is at the heart of the attraction and formation of personal experiences. Obviously, not everything we think, dream, or imagine turns into a physical event. There are a number of factors which go together to determine just which events will come to physical manifestation.

In the first place, the powers of creation do not lie in the hands of the private ego. Remember that the ego, or the private sense of self, is but a partial expression of the greater, more encompassing Self. Although the ego may forget that it is dependent upon a vast, multidimensional gestalt of consciousness, it is still in a relatively subsidiary position. If efforts to create or form physical experiences and events in certain ways are not in keeping with the deeper purposes of the Self, then those efforts may be thwarted by a higher authority, so to speak. For example, in some cases an individual may remain poor despite his or her desires because the Self knows that individual is not ready to handle wealth responsibly. Furthermore, certain experiences and life-situations are brought about by the Self to educate the aspect of self, centered around the ego. But to the degree that the private self's efforts are in basic accord with the higher Self's designs, the private self has freedom in shaping its own experiences. In such cases the private self becomes the architect, as it were, directing the forces of creation into those channels which lead to the formation of physical events. But even in these cases, there are factors which play a critical role in determining the relative likelihood of a mental event becoming a physical event.

The intensity of a mental structure or event is critical. Strong emotional energy, intensity of focus, duration of mental energies—these and other factors determine the intensity of a mental pattern. Any level of mental energy may be communicated to the physical dimension, but it takes a certain amount of power for those energies to effectively alter the physical environment. If this were not the case, physical reality would be like certain regions of the dream environment where the thoughts and feelings of the dreamer are instantaneously embodied in energy structures.

Clarity in a mental event is also critical. Physical structures have definite boundaries and are measurable. If a mental event is fuzzy, if the intent behind it is wavering, or if the structure is less than clearly defined, then physical energies cannot clearly organize about it.

As we have already seen, a multitude of factors affects the intensity and clarity of any thought-form or mental event. Conflicting mental patterns can drain it of energy. Operational belief structures which negate it can completely cut off its possibilities of physical manifestation. Competing mental energies and desires can diffuse one's focus, so that a single thought-form never attains the critically necessary energy level. Doubts and lack of determination can also continually drain the energy levels.

Obviously, though, we do have physical experiences. Many of our mental patterns are of such a long-standing and energized nature that they effectively materialize. We establish an overriding group of mental structures that form a basic pattern to our experiences. This is why many of our experiences are similar in nature. However, when we try to interject the new or the unusual, we may find difficulty in manifesting the mental structures physically.

If you consistently have a strong attitude of insecurity, you attract experiences that express and reinforce the patterns of insecurity. If you have a consistent belief that you are poor, then your poverty remains or increases. Basic, consistent beliefs and mental patterns, along with the overriding purposes of the higher Self, establish the core of our experiences. Those who strongly believe in their capacity for creating wealth will continually make money. Those who have always believed they were social outcasts will always have difficulty in making friends. Your day-to-day beliefs, attitudes, thoughts, and feelings produce the energy patterns around which a majority of your physical experiences form. And of course any belief, limiting or otherwise, may be altered, as discussed in Chapter 4.

Physical Events and Collective Mental Energies

The world we live in is a collective venture. None of our experiences exist in a vacuum. Everything we do is interwoven with what everyone else does. You may love someone and strongly desire that he or she love you. But your efforts cannot force another person to comply. Just as you attract your own chosen events, so do others. If what you want manifested involves other people, then their intentions and purposes must be taken into consideration.

On a wider scale, the amassed mental energies of a nation determine the public events that take place in that nation. If a nation goes to war it is never because one person or a small group of people unilaterally made the decision in favor of war. It is because the group psyche so wills it, and a few individuals set into motion that group will.

At times we may feel that the course of human events is so overwhelming that we as individuals can have no effect. We think that we are powerless to affect the course of history. The powers that be seem to have all control. But every individual plays a part in the formation of public events. There can be no economic depression in a nation, for example, unless the weight of the national mind creates it.

The same holds true on a worldwide scale. Any event that affects the lives of everyone on the planet must have been created through the mental energies of all people. In one way or another, we are all responsible for every war that breaks out. We are equally responsible for each new, great, positive movement.

Advances come about when the combined mental energies of all those on the planet dictate that the time is ripe. Obviously, not all of this takes place on a conscious level.

All events are nonphysical before they are physical. The private physical events of each individual interact with the private events of everyone else. This interblending sets the stage for public events. And public events reverberate back to the individual and affect his or her private events. But we all have some influence on which events will occur and which ones won't.

THE CREATION OF REALITY

To say that our experience of reality is the sum of the succession of the events we create would be too simple. The dance of consciousness is far too complex to be seen in such a straightforward manner. As event follows event, each experience we manifest affects us and our perception of reality. Adjustments are made continually. We have successes and failures, and hopefully we learn from all of them. Through all of it we are guided and taught by the more encompassing aspect of ourselves—the Self, which is who and what we are beyond the limitations of our physical focus.

Not all mental patterns are formed for the purposes of eventual physical manifestation. Many serve to color our perceptions regarding events we experience. Our attitudes and moods act as energy filters through which we perceive reality. Through them the same event may be perceived as positive or negative, depressing or inspirational. Expectations and desires affect what we perceive. Likewise, when we compare our mental ideals with physical actuality, we emotionally and intellectually alter our perceptions to fit the ideals.

We forget or never knew the the part we play in forming the events that unfold before us. We project our creativity into outside forces and say that these events are happening *to* us, rather than considering that they may unfold out of us. Our beliefs may lead us to attribute events to patterns of cause and effect which may be irrelevant.

All of this mental and physical interplay involves a constant flow of energies between dimensions. We may initiate events and then put a restraining order on them. We may set up mental patterns that, when manifested before our eyes, cause us to wish we had never started them. We sometimes desire something, but when we get it we don't want it and wonder why we did in the first place. We work hard to create a certain pattern of life for ourselves and then get bored with it. Can we change things once the forces are set into motion? I believe we change the course of our experiences by changing our mental patterns through conscious effort.

These complex fluctuations and interweavings between dimensions and within each dimension become even more complex when we consider the vast field of consciousness within which we operate. Our thoughts, feelings, actions, and experiences blend and interact with the same types of energies emerging from everyone else. We agree; we disagree. We work together; we work against each other. We each observe history and then we psychically debate over what should be done about it and about the course humankind should pursue.

But even though it all seems to be a complicated

mess, the wonder is that it is a perfectly operating system. In the vast reaches of mental space we may battle like the gods of Olympus, but life and the evolution of consciousness go on. We are wiser and more powerful than we know. We have before us the task of incorporating this inner wisdom and power into our current focus of consciousness.

We are still experimenting and playing with our powers of creativity. This world, with its linear time, is a school where our creations develop slowly so that we can see what we are doing and evolve into the wisdom of the Self. The forces we generate are spread out and slowed down so that we can witness the effects of our mental patterns. Time allows us to make adjustments and corrections. Our social venture allows us to learn cooperation.

It should be clear by now that our mental patterns help to determine the events we encounter physically. Events run together to form the stream of our life. Each life with the events in it interweaves with the lives of everyone else to form the history of humankind. If we do not shape our experiences consciously, then we will do it from blind habit. At each moment we can choose whether to be aware of what we are helping to create. Sooner or later we must realize what we are doing. With that realization comes great power, and great responsibility.

The exploration of the nature of the processes of mind and creativity, however, becomes more complex before it becomes simpler. In the next chapter I hope to demonstrate through some of the findings of physicists how the mind deals with the complexity of reality. Many of the concepts discussed thus far may seem to contradict or defy the known laws of nature. But as will be seen shortly, our understanding of the laws of nature is undergoing a major revolution, a revolution which has not yet filtered its way into the minds of the general populace. Nevertheless, physical science is beginning to produce evidence of the preeminence of mind in the formation of reality.

8

The Physics of Mind

If thoughts, mental patterns, and mental events are objective realities, there should be some evidence in physical reality to affirm this fact. If mental reality plays an important part in the structuring and ordering of our physical world, there must be a point at which the blending or meeting of dimensions takes place. It would seem that sooner or later even the most physical of the physical sciences must bear witness to the importance of mind.

Early in this century physicists began exploring the world of the infinitesimally small. At the very beginning of these explorations they discovered that the world is very different from what was previously supposed. Heisenberg, Lorentz, Einstein, Wheeler, and other great physicists have since led the way toward revolutionary ways of thinking about the nature of time, space, and reality. By studying the behavior of the smallest traceable components of physical reality, they have found themselves standing irrevocably on the threshold of other dimensions.

QUANTUM PHYSICS AND THE NATURE OF MIND

Until early in the twentieth century it was believed that physical reality was constructed of tiny building blocks of matter. The atom was considered to be the smallest building block of matter. As methods of scientific observation improved, and as more penetrating minds were focused on the issue, it became clear that atoms themselves are composed of even smaller units. Subatomic particles were discovered, and they became the supposed essential building blocks.

As physicists studied these subatomic particles, strange anomalies began to appear. Although at times these tiny units behaved as particles, at other times they behaved more like waves of energy. Furthermore, even when they behaved like particles, they exhibited some startling characteristics.

The Indeterminate World of the Quantum and the Observer

Physicist Werner Heisenberg, now famous for the Heisenberg Uncertainty Principle, discovered the first of these anomalies in the world of the infinitesimally small. He discovered that electrons cannot be isolated, that in essence they refuse to submit to a comprehensive physical gaze. His experiments showed that if you locate an electron in space, you cannot simultaneously determine its direction or speed. On the other hand, if you determine the speed and direction of an electron, you cannot then know its position in space. You can have one or the other, but you cannot simultaneously determine both.

On first consideration this may not seem to be a very important finding. But from the point of view of physicists, who study the nature of physical reality, it had some unsettling effects. Here was a constituent part of matter that refused to obey the long-established rules of nature. Therefore, an element of uncertainty was introduced into the picture. On the subatomic level there would always be at least one factor that refused to be pinned down and would remain unknowable.

Next came the dilemma of particles, waves, and the nature of light. As early as 1801 Thomas Young, an English physicist, showed that light has wave-like properties. He passed light through two slits in an opaque sheet onto another surface. You would expect to see two bars of light falling on the surface, as would happen if light were composed of particles. Instead there were several bars of light, indicating a wave interference pattern. This conflicted with the traditional view that light is composed of energetic particles.[1]

For a while it was accepted that light is composed of waves. But around the turn of the century physicists Albert Einstein and Max Planck renewed the debate by demonstrating that light seemed to be neither waves nor particles but tiny packets of energy which could exhibit properties of either waves or particles. These packets of light-energy came to be called photons. This might have settled the issue if later experiments had not further complicated matters.

Early in this century it became possible to control light to the point that one photon at a time could be shot onto a photographic plate, where it would leave a mark or spot. With this new technique physicists again performed the double-slit experiment. By releasing one photon at a time, they could see each spot as it developed. It was seen that each photon went through either one slit or the other, just like any projected particle would. But eventually, after enough photons were released, the old pattern of several bars of light appeared.

This experiment raises the question: If the photons pass through the slits one at a time and pass through only one slit, how is it that they form an interference pattern? Passing through one at a time, photons should not interfere with each other and should behave like particles. But the results suggest that each photon somehow "knew" that there would be others and that it had to behave as if it were interacting with those others. The explanation given for this anomaly by quantum physics makes the picture even more strange.

According to quantum physics each photon actually passes through both slits at the same time. Doing this it "knows" that there are two open slits, thus necessitating an interference pattern. In order to pass through both slits simultaneously, the photon cannot exist as a single object while it is in transit. During the phase of its transit the photon seems to be able to manifest itself as more than one probabilistic counterpart of itself, thereby exploring all possible pathways open to it. Only when it reaches the photographic plate does it abandon these multiple existences and return to behaving like a single particle.

The conclusion is that subatomic "particles" exist in a state of probabilities. In this state they may be in more than one place at the same time. Then, depending on the conditions established by an observer, they may "choose" where and how they focus into a single event or phenomenon.

Because this concept is so important to the issue at hand, I want to give one more startling example. Scientists have observed the behavior of photons emitted from distant quasars (star-like celestial objects that emit radio waves), particularly those that passed by an intervening galaxy on their flight to us. A galaxy has a tremendous overall gravitational effect. A particle-detecting device reveals that each photon is made to veer to the right or the left by the gravitational pull of the galaxy. It registers on the particle-detecting device as a spot, demonstrating its particle nature. But if a wave-detecting device is used to register these on-coming photons, each photon is shown to pass on both sides of the galaxy and subsequently establish a wave-interference pattern.

Now these photons, according to our understanding of the universe, must have been emitted many light years ago. Yet we are able to determine whether they behaved as particles or as waves when they passed the galaxy so long ago. It seems that through the simple process of choice and observation we are able to influence past events.

To summarize: Quantum physics tells us that sub-atomic particles exist in an indeterminate state of prob-abilities, each probability representing one of the many different manifestations that each particle could take. These particles do not step out of their fog of prob-abilities until an observer enters the picture and chooses which probability he or she wishes to see manifested. If we want to see a photon behave like a particle, we project it through a single opening. If we wish to see it behave like a wave, we give it two or more openings to go through. In each case it will com-ply. In other words, at the nonphysical level of real-ity photons exist as both particles and waves, but when they manifest physically they must do so as either waves or particles. In the experiments of quantum physicists it is demonstrated that the observer deter-mines which way a particular photon will manifest.

The generally accepted conclusion from the findings of quantum physics is that at the quantum level real-ity is indeterminate and fuzzy.[2] If we look closely at the basic structure of reality, we find that things ex-ist in a state of hazy, unmanifest probabilities. In essence, at this level, reality as we know it does not yet physically exist. It takes on the normally accepted characteristics of physical materialization only when an observer enters the picture. It seems that consciousness and mind focus this indeterminancy into an observable picture of reality.

I believe this is the scientists' first recognition of what might be called the threshold between physical and nonphysical reality. It brings to mind how our mental patterns, events, and decisions hold the potential for several paths of action. Eventually we choose one of these and implement it in physical reality. Could this be essentially the same process whereby indeterminate, nonphysical energy, existing in a state of probabilities, is translated into an isolated manifestation according to the choice of an observer?

Probabilities, Variations, and the Many Worlds Hypothesis

Consider that each quantum, or each infinitesimally small packet of energy, exists in a state of multiple probabilities out of which only one is made physically manifest. What happens with the unmanifest probabilities? As with most things in the realm of the new physics, there is no total agreement in regard to the answer to this question, and two basic schools of thought have developed.

According to what is known as the Copenhagen interpretation, the probability or potential for reality that did not manifest existed only as a statistical or mathematical reality, and in fact never had any objective reality to begin with.[3] In my opinion this view does not truly address the issue; it only skirts it in an attempt to avoid it. The actual equations of quantum mechanics demonstrate no support for the Copenhagen interpretation. As author Michael Talbot says, "To say that one is only a statistical reality is thus arbitrary, an after-the-fact assumption based on our own internal bias, but not on anything inherent in the mathematics of quantum physics."[4]

The other school of thought has come to involve what is known as "the many worlds hypothesis," originated by physicists John A. Wheeler and Hugh Everett. According to the proponents of this school of thought, the unmanifest probabilities actually branch off into parallel universes which are inaccessible to our physical senses. Every quantum event therefore implies a number of parallel dimensions or systems in which each physically unmanifest probability is manifested. Considering the nearly infinite number of quantum events that go into making up the structure of our physical universe, this suggests a staggering number of unperceived probabilities existing in an equally staggering number of parallel universes.

We have been looking exclusively at the behavior of subatomic particles and quanta. But it must be remembered that everything we physically perceive is made up of these tiny elements. Each object involves countless quantum events; every physical event rests on countless objects, forces, and aspects of physical reality. So every event in our lives involves a nearly infinite number of quantum events. This means that at the heart of every event we experience, there exists this same indeterminacy and condition of probabilities.

For a moment let's look at it from the other direction. We discussed earlier how every aspect of consciousness seeks to express itself in as many ways as possible. In the case of a thought-form, the consciousness behind the energy composing that thought-form seeks complete expression. Therefore, inherent within and springing from the single thought-form are all the variations of that thought. Every mental event ripples outward into nonphysical space, each ripple corresponding to a variation on the original theme.

To illustrate this, imagine that you are trying to decide between taking a college class in psychology and one in history. Now to you, those are the only two possibilities that matter, so they are the only ones you will think about. But if you wanted to, you could find quite a number of other possibilities inherent in this basic choice. You could, for example, take no class at all. You could take both. You could take some other class altogether. You could take one now and the other later. Such variations on the original theme go on endlessly.

This tendency toward infinite variations threads its way through all aspects of reality. Quantum events, physical events, thoughts, emotions, and mental events—all of these generate countless possible variations, and we assume that each of the variations exists somewhere, in some dimension. On a grander scale this would mean that there are countless Earths, each with some connection to the one we know, but each with some difference. One Earth may have no people, and one may be just like ours but with no wars. You can explore the possibilities as well as I can.

So you can see that we are returning to the concept of sorting through mental events in order to determine which ones will be selected for physical actualization. In my opinion observer participation on the quantum level indicates the physical mechanics of this process. Fortunately we don't have to deal with such minute intricacies at the conscious level. As we deal with events on a larger scale, energy and the cooperating aspects of consciousness take care of the mechanics on the structural level. You can see that life involves us in an unceasing process of consciously making choices, which further involves us in drawing from a vast bank of probabilities and possibilities in order to create or manifest the experience of reality we want.

Black Holes, White Holes, and Interdimensional Doorways

There is one other aspect of quantum physics which might provide us with a better understanding of this interplay between dimensions of reality. However, some background is necessary before we go into this. Albert Einstein, through his revolutionary work in the field of relativity, demonstrated that space and time are not separate parameters of physical reality but are in fact combined into one interdependent parameter which is now called simply "space-time." According to his findings, space and time are really one, and to affect one is to affect the other. This interdependence is most clearly demonstrated in regions of the space-time fabric called black holes.

In and around black holes physicists encounter some amazing surprises, or what they call singularities. According to Fred Alan Wolf, physicist and author: "At a singularity, all physical quantities take on infinite values. These singularities exist at the centers of objects called black holes. In these black holes, space and time become highly stretched. Time intervals stretch so much that light slows down to zero speed as it approaches one. In other words, light stops moving at the center of a black hole, and the laws of physics go crazy. In the vicinity of these distortions there are gateways to other universes." [5]

Einstein's General Theory of Relativity does predict distortions of space and time in the region of strong gravitational forces. Within a black hole it seems that great mass is compressed to a small volume, resulting in phenomenal gravitational forces. In fact, as Wolf stated, mathematical analysis indicates that at the center of a black hole mass reaches infinity. The gravitational effect at such points is so strong that light cannot escape, thus the name "black hole."

The mathematical and statistical equations pertaining to the properties of a black hole are beyond the scope of this book. I will attempt to detail them from a lay point of view. Those wishing a deeper understanding can read books such as *Relativity* by Albert Einstein or *Mathematical Foundations of Quantum Theory*, edited by A. R. Marlow.

According to Einstein's view, the speed of light is a constant. Nothing can go faster than the speed of light, and the speed at which light travels does not change. In a black hole, however, the speed of light appears to drop to zero. The particles or quanta in the light are trapped by the black hole's gravitational forces. So we have infinite mass bringing light to a standstill.

Now, imagine you are watching someone approach a black hole. If he or she points a flashing beam of light in your direction, you would see the flashes of light appearing gradually farther and farther apart. From your point of view, slowing the light has the effect of slowing time. The person with the light would notice no difference, but you would see the flashes slow down until you could not see them at all. From our point of view, time slows down near a black hole.

Quantum physics tells us that time, as we know it, actually stops completely at the center of a black hole. Further, quantum equations indicate that there is a flip side to these black holes; as an object passes through such holes time actually undergoes a reversal, at least from our point of view. In other words, a black hole may serve as a portal to time reversal.

This concept is difficult to convey, as it upsets basic beliefs about time and space. But in essence, according to quantum physics, in black holes our physical laws break down and a different dimension exists. Mathematically, it appears that time and space are transcended at such points. Theoretically, an object leaving the physical universe through a black hole could reemerge at any point in time and space, if it reemerges at all.

I suspect physicists will soon come across "white" holes, though to my knowledge they have not yet been discovered. White holes would be the opposite of black holes; while matter and energy *exit* our physical system through black holes, matter and energy would *enter* our system in the vicinity of white holes. In combination these holes would constitute points at which parallel universes and adjacent dimensions touch. The question naturally arises, where are these holes?

According to Wolf, any bit of subatomic matter may be able to form infinitesimally small black and white holes. It is possible that at nearly every point other dimensions of reality impinge upon physical reality. As Wolf states, "In particular, the spinning bits of matter called electrons may be dense enough to be black holes. If so, they lead to an infinite number of parallel universes, since all black holes lead to parallel universes." [6]

The main point I want to make is that there is physical evidence to support the contention that "nonphysical" reality interconnects with physical reality at virtually every point. At these points physical reality appears and disappears continuously, as probabilities come into physical manifestation or not. These "holes" are interdimensional doorways through which time and space are transcended and through which energy is capable of passing. Of course, the nature of that energy changes when such passages are made.

In my opinion physics seems to demonstrate that every event is first a bank of nonphysical probabilities. Second, it requires consciousness, or an observer, to select one probability for physical manifestation. Third, black holes and theoretical white holes display properties which indicate that they serve as doorways between parallel universes or alternate dimensions. And finally, if you put it all together, it seems as if this physical dimension is constantly emerging into existence at every point, out of nonphysical dimensions, and that consciousness and mind determine the shape this reality takes at each moment.

ONE WORLD, ONE MIND

We now believe that every perceptible object and event is composed of a vast multitude of subatomic particles and packets of energy. This being the case, how do these particles come together in such a way as to organize themselves in a consistent structure in accordance with the mental energies, or with the intentions of a higher consciousness, calling for the particular event? In other words, how do these minute particles communicate with one another, if this is in fact what they do?

In the West we have traditionally viewed the world as composed of a nearly infinite number of separate parts. These parts, furthermore, are considered to be able to influence each other under the right conditions. For such influences to take place, there must be some observable intervening connection, force, or causal relationship. All such influences and interactions take place not only across distance, but also over the course of time. But the type of communication that would be required for mental events to form physical events would have to be instantaneous in nature. A whole system of aggregate parts must simultaneously "agree" on the operations they will perform.

Is the traditional Western view of the world accurate? Must all cause and effect transpire in time? Do influences have to pass through some intervening space? Or is there a communication network in the universe that transcends time and space?

The Transcendence of Time and Space

We have already seen how the observer influences that which is observed, especially in the realm of quantum actions. Referring back to that, experiments have been performed in which a molecule containing two atoms, and with a net spin of zero, has been allowed to break apart. Due to the net spin of zero, the two atoms each continue to spin, but their relative directional spin must still add up to zero: they must spin in opposite directions. Now, remembering the part an observer plays, an apparatus can be situated arbitrarily so that in one case atom A will be seen to spin in one direction, necessitating a spin in the other direction on the part of atom B. If the apparatus is then situated in another position, atom A will be observed to spin in a new direction, and atom B will also reorient its spin to cancel atom A.

The question is: how does atom B know when we have altered the apparatus and the resulting spin of atom A? If they are far enough apart, there can be no intervening causal relationship, at least not in the classical sense. According to David Bohm, professor of theoretical physics at Birbeck College in London:

"This change is somehow transmitted *immediately* to atom B, which responds accordingly. Thus, we are led to contradict one of the basic principles of the theory of relativity, which states that no physical influences can be propagated faster than light." [7]

Even light, the fastest known thing in the physical universe, takes time to traverse space. But here we have a case of instantaneous communication. This anomaly, and the one involving photons communicating their "decision" to behave as either waves or particles, have led many physicists, including David Bohm and the late Niels Bohr, to propose the existence of a nonlocal system of reality. As mentioned briefly, a nonlocal system of reality is one in which neither time nor space limits the communications or influences between two or more events. In other words, we are faced with a dimension of reality in which events can have effects upon each other across any distance in zero time.

Such discoveries imply that every part of the universe may be capable of instantaneously communicating with every other part. Distance means nothing; time delay is nonexistent. Such a phenomenon inevitably leads us in the direction of considering that our Western view of the world, wherein the universe consists of distinct and separate parts, is in error. We must consider the possibility that the universe is so intricately interconnected that it can only be considered as one working whole.

Total Interconnectedness

In Eastern philosophies and religions, the doctrine of the unity of the universe is pervasive. Until this century, however, there was no scientific evidence to support a doctrine of unity. Things are changing.

Albert Einstein was probably the first to propose a scientific basis for the unity of the universe. His General Theory of Relativity sprang from his attempts to do this. Working from his understanding of the dynamics of gravity, space, and time, and taking into consideration the new discoveries in the field of quantum mechanics, he proposed what he called the Unified Field Theory.

According to Bohm, "He [Einstein] took the total field of the whole universe as a primary description. This field is continuous and indivisible. Particles are then to be regarded as certain kinds of abstractions from the total field, corresponding to regions of very intense field (called singularities). As the distance from the singularity increases, the field gets weaker, until it merges imperceptibly with the fields of other singularities. But nowhere is there a break or division. Thus, the classical idea of the separability of the world into distinct but interacting parts is no longer valid or relevant. Rather, we have to regard the universe as *an undivided and unbroken whole.*" [8]

So according to Einstein's Unified Field Theory, the entire universe consists of one vast field of energy. The activities at one point have some effect on the activities at every other point. You are not separate from what you perceive to be outside yourself. Essential separateness is an illusion.

The Unified Field Theory is not the only area in which science is coming to see the unity of all things. The phenomenon of observer participancy on the quantum level and the nonlocal system of reality of quantum mechanics also point the way to this concept. Instantaneous communication at the quantum level opens the way for total interconnectedness. Once again from Bohm we hear: "A centrally relevant change in descriptive order required in the quantum theory is thus the dropping of the notion of analysis of the world into relatively autonomous parts, separately existent but in interaction. Rather, the primary emphasis is now on undivided wholeness, in which the observing instrument is not separable from what is observed." [9]

It seems that the universe is constructed in a manner far different from our traditional view. All parts are connected to all other parts; every part influences every other part. On some levels these influences take place instantaneously. If the mental energy of an individual is part of this field of energy, is it any wonder that telepathy can occur instantaneously across vast distances? It becomes possible to see how our mental energies, in conjunction with our greater Self, can arrange wide-ranging events in such a way as to perfectly manifest the experiences necessary to us from moment to moment. Does this view leave any room for accidents?

The Universal Hologram

We will look at one more scientific view of the nature of the universe, one that is in accord with the preceding material. In this view the universe is pictured as a giant hologram, or three-dimensional photograph. An object may be photographed from all directions with a laser beam, and the resulting photographic image, when projected into space, appears as three-dimensional. One can walk around such a holographic image and see it from every view, just as if it were a solid, three-dimensional object.

Holographic pictures have a strange characteristic. If the film containing a holographic image is cut into several pieces, each piece contains the entire image. Cut those pieces into smaller pieces, and the smaller pieces also contain the whole image.

Bohm's findings in regard to the nonlocal system of reality have led him to propose a holographic model of the universe. Because of the interdimensional access of each part of the universe to every other part, each part in essence contains the whole. As Bohm sees it, just as in a hologram each part interpenetrates all the other parts, in a nonlocal universe every part interpenetrates every other part.[10]

Working from a different direction, Stanford neurophysiologist Karl Pribram also proposed a holographic model of the universe. He found that the brain works like a hologram. Neurophysiologist Karl Lashley discovered that when an individual suffered damage to a portion of the brain, often he or she could still perform functions that were controlled by that portion. It has also been found that memory cannot be isolated in the brain. Regardless of the portion of the brain that is damaged or removed, memory can be recovered. Pribram interprets these phenomena as demonstrating that the functions of memory are not located in any particular portion of the brain, but are distributed throughout the whole brain. This is reminiscent of the way images interpenetrate a hologram. Pribram proposes that even our physical world may be a hologram.[11]

Author Michael Talbot sums up Pribram's postulations in this way: "Even at a level available to our perceptions, objective reality is holographic and might be thought of as little more than a "frequency domain." That is, even the world we know may not be composed of objects. We may only be sensing mechanisms moving through a vibrating dance of frequencies. Pribram suggests that the reason we translate this vibrating dance of frequencies into the solidity and objectivity of the universe as we know it is that our brains operate on the same holographic-like principles as the dance of frequencies and are able to convert them into a picture much the same as a television converts the frequencies it receives into a more coherent image." [12]

The holographic model of the universe provides us with one more viable way of seeing the interconnectedness of its myriad parts. The apparent unity and interrelatedness of all things add to the plausibility of experience as we know it originating in mental dimensions. It suggests this by giving a reasonable explanation of how each mind may be simultaneously in touch with all available probabilities in any given situation, thereby allowing each mind to select for manifestation a series of experiences out of an infinite number of possible choices. I believe that evidence is mounting in support of the preeminence of mind and consciousness in the construction of reality. In the final analysis, it seems that the line dividing physical reality from nonphysical reality does not exist at all.

Morphogenetic Fields and the Group Mind

So far we have been looking at the interpenetration of reality by all of its constituent parts primarily from a physical point of view. But there are also scientists who have found evidence indicating that such interconnectedness and interpenetration occur on the mental level. One of these scientists is plant physiologist Rupert Sheldrake.

Sheldrake proposes a mysterious force field that connects each member of a species with all of the past members of that species. He also proposes that each species has a "group mind" which unites and connects all of its members psychically. He bases these propositions on discoveries in the field of biological research.[13]

The concept of morphogenetic fields was originally proposed by two embryologists in the 1920s, Alexander Gurwitsch and Paul Weiss, but they did not develop it thoroughly. Sheldrake proposes that these fields of energy govern the behavior of living organisms. He asserts that the experiences of members of one species are somehow transmitted to future members of that species.

Sheldrake cites experiments of Harvard psychologist William McDougall in support of these contentions. These experiments involved rats in a complicated maze. McDougall found that each succeeding generation of rats learned to navigate the maze more quickly than the one before. He used different genetic strains of rats to eliminate the possibility that the information was transmitted genetically. The results indicate that as a species the rats partook of the experience of past members of the species.

This is not the only basis for Sheldrake's proposals. Studies in genetics, embryology, and microbiology give further evidence that through some nonphysical energy field members within a species are able to learn from one another independently of time and space. Such phenomena led Sheldrake to propose the existence of a group mind for each species, a bank of mental experience available to each member.

The concept of morphogenetic fields not only supports the theory of the total interpenetration of all parts of the universe, including individual minds; it also gives strong evidence of some form of telepathy transcending the boundaries of time and space. The traditional limitations of reality which we have believed in for so long are being challenged on many fronts. Time and space have a limited domain. Consciousness and mind are seen to carry far more importance than we thought.

Hopefully, this chapter has shown that there is strong evidence in support of the concepts of the interconnectedness of all aspects of reality, and that the mind and consciousness are the preeminent determining factors in the shaping of the reality we perceive. But science, by its very nature, must move slowly. We do not have to wait for scientists to confirm the existence of every avenue of reality before we investigate it. The nature of reality has been explored from many directions besides that taken by Western science. In the next chapter I return to considering aspects of mind and consciousness not yet probed by science.

9

The Extended Reach of Mind and Self

Because of our narrow focus in one dimension of reality, and because we are so involved in day-to-day activities, we tend to think of ourselves as quite limited and contained. Our whole existence at times seems to be centered around our bodies. Most people, if asked where their center of consciousness is located, would say that it is in their heads. We seem to have a very distinct notion we are an island of consciousness, separate from everything else "out there."

Is this self, this personality which says "I am," all there is? Are we as simple as we appear when we look only at the obvious portion of ourselves? Or are there greater dimensions to our being? If subatomic particles, events, and mental patterns are multidimensional, is it possible that we alone are one-dimensional?

ASPECT SELVES

We have seen how each constituent part of the physical dimension exists primarily as a nonphysical bank of probabilities and potentialities. We have considered the possibility that in another dimension every particle and event manifests itself in a wide variety of ways. There they may take on a number of different forms, functions, and patterns of behavior. When they manifest physically, they show a single face or form of the many that could just as easily have been manifested. Their other forms or faces remain unmanifest from our point of view, but fully manifest and functioning within a dimension beyond the range of our physical senses.

You and I are no less events than an atom or a tree. To say that we "are" is somewhat inappropriate. "To be" or the state of "being" implies a fixity, a stasis. But we are always in a state of becoming; the essence of our nature is change. We continually "happen." Since we, too, are events which may take their course in any number of different ways, is it not reasonable to assume that we may be manifest in another dimension, in a wide variety of guises? Is it not reasonable to expect that the single individual which you know as "you" is but one manifestation of the potential selves which are physically unmanifested but nonphysically quite real?

What would these other aspects and dimensions of our selves be like? Are they really a part of us? Do they lessen the significance of that being we think we are, or do they enhance it? Can we in fact come to know ourselves as encompassing all of these wide-ranging aspects and faces?

Probable Events and Probable Selves

Each moment of our lives involves us in the making of decisions. Some of these decisions are conscious and some are relatively unconscious. Previously we saw how we weigh alternatives within the mind. Mental events are created to correspond to our options. Out of those mentally surveyed options, we select one and attempt to implement it as an active force in our physical lives.

When you try to decide between staying at home or going to a movie, you rapidly envision yourself taking each path. But what happens to the mental event you do not choose? If you stay at home, then the choice of going to a movie effectually disappears from your conscious awareness. But does this mean that it altogether ceases to exist?

Each idea or mental pattern, upon its formation or creation, is imbued with the impetus to continue. As we saw earlier, consciousness underlies its energy, and due to its inherent nature, consciousness seeks to pursue the path of expression. Obviously, some degree of consciousness is involved in each mental event or idea you formulate.

Now, the mental events corresponding to options you consider in making a decision have this impetus to proceed on the path of manifestation. One of them, by your choice, is propelled into physical manifestation. The other mental event or events not chosen do not magically cease to exist. They continue to unfold according to their nature, whether or not you choose to participate consciously in that process of unfoldment. At some level of reality each mental event evolves along its own natural course. The unchosen events branch off from your main line of action and take place in other dimensions of reality.

I know this is a difficult concept to understand, but I will try to simplify it. Each of us has memories of crucial points in our lives which involved us in major decisions. Perhaps when you were younger you were in love with someone, but in the course of time you grew apart and separated. Maybe from time to time you wonder what your life would have been like if you had married that person. From your current point of view you are considering a probable reality scenario which you did not choose. So, what I am saying is that at some level of reality you did marry that person and your life proceeded on that basis.

The same principle holds with all your major decisions. Somewhere in reality you did take the job that in this reality you turned down. In some dimension you did not choose your present career but that other career you once thought about pursuing. At another level of reality you pursued every critical course of action you might have pursued physically but did not.

On the same note, every decision that involves you in sorting probabilities and in choosing a path initiates the progression of every option, at some level of reality. Each moment-point of your life rises into physical existence out of a bank of probabilities. Those probabilities do not cease to exist simply because you do not choose them for physical manifestation. In fact, just about anywhere along the line you may change your mind about something, reject your original choice, and through reselection actualize one of those other probabilities.

Naturally, scenarios not acted upon do not become part of what you think of as your central existence. But neither do they totally cease to be a part of you. You were involved in their original inception, and however briefly, your consciousness was interwoven with them. Therefore, however these nonphysical scenarios or probabilities proceed, there is still a connection between you and them. Psychic and mental energies remain to connect you with all the paths you could have manifested but did not.

So it would seem that there are a multitude of "yous" pursuing every possible path of action. This is consistent with the propensity of consciousness to express itself in as wide a variety of ways as possible. The nature of this physical system of reality limits our expression of our inner natures, but in other dimensions of reality every possible aspect of you is expressed.

These other "yous," however, take on a life of their own. By your own choice you cease to be the governing consciousness behind them. Still, there is consciousness within the energy which originally composed them on the mental level. This consciousness has become a gestalt on its own and follows through with the original impetus. So in a sense these other diverging scenarios are a part of you, but at the same time they are not you.

It is quite possible for you to obtain subjective evidence that these probable selves and events exist. Because of the original and continuing connection between your current focus of consciousness and these probable selves, a mental pathway remains between you and them. Think about some road that you chose not to take in your life. In imagination place yourself upon this road. Then try to sense, feel, and see what develops. You may be surprised at the vividness with which images and feelings come. You will be effectually attuning yourself to these separate but connected probable selves, and you can share in their experiences.

Hopefully, as we proceed with investigating other ways in which our consciousness is involved with probabilities, this concept will make more sense to you. Bear in mind that you are a multidimensional being and that your full nature is too vast to be expressed within the confines of a single reality system. Your current, physical life merely expresses one possible line of development.

The Dreaming Self and Probabilites

One way of better understanding how a primary focus of consciousness interacts with probabilities is through looking at some of the activities of the dreaming self. When you dream, your conscious focus is turned toward the nonphysical realms and therefore is not bound by the usual restrictions of time and space. Without such restrictions, it is easier for consciousness to express more of its manifold properties.

To begin with, while dreaming you may take on any form or appearance you choose. You may explore facets of reality as a member of either sex, as a member of any race, or as an individual of any age. You can be strong or weak, tall or short, fat or thin. You can, in fact, operate through any form that you can imagine.

No matter what appearance you take on while dreaming, you are still you. The consciousness behind these changing forms remains the same; only the external manifestation changes. Each external appearance, however, represents a probable version of your own self-expression.

Just as the dreaming self can manifest a wide variety of appearances, it can also enact a multitude of dreaming scenarios. For the purposes of decision-making, you can play out every option you perceive to be available to you in the situation. Out of this experimentation you can select the path you want to take in physical reality.

The dreaming focus of consciousness explores probabilities in a similar manner. Given its inherent freedom within the nonphysical dimension, the dreaming focus is not limited to the expression of a single probability; it is free to manifest and explore every probability. Within the realm of the dreamer's activities, each probability scenario is just as valid and real as any other probability. They all validly express the inherent nature of the individual consciousness.

Finally, your dreaming focus of consciousness is itself an alternate or probable version of you. While you are awake, your physical focus of consciousness is the one you deem most real and valid. But when you dream, the dreaming focus of consciousness maintains the primary reality, and at such times the waking focus is alternate, probable, and subsidiary. Obviously, when you are awake and operating in physical reality, you do not manifest your dreaming focus. It would be out of place and could not function in the relatively limited physical domain. The dreaming focus becomes an unmanifest, probable version of who you are, at least from the point of view of your physical focus. Your attention determines which parts of you are considered primary and which are considered probabilities.

Reincarnational Selves and Counterparts

As mentioned in Chapter 2, the private self with which each of us primarily identifies is but a partial expression or manifestation of our total Self. The Self is that vast gestalt of consciousness that transcends our current notions of identity and awareness but remains our deeper, truer identity. Limited by the parameters of the physical dimension, the Self cannot approach a full expression of itself through one incarnation or life on earth. One lifetime and one personality structure can serve to express only a few of its many facets. Similarly, it is impossible to express yourself through only one role: you may be a parent, a son or daughter, an employee or professional person, a part-time artist, and a friend to others, all at the same time. Each of these roles serves to express only a portion of who and what you are.

In order for the Self to express its fuller nature in human terms, it must pursue a course of many lives. Remember that when I speak of the Self I am speaking of who you are in a greater context. So, "you" may explore intellectuality in the persona of a woman in the sixteenth century. You as the Self may explore emotional intensity as a male dancer in the seventeenth century. You may express creativity and artistic abilities as a personality during the Renaissance. You as the Self may explore the struggle for survival as a prehistoric caveman. In each of these succeeding incarnations, as viewed from the perspective of linear time, different aspects of your Self are expressed in physical terms. In the course of time, then, the Self comes to know itself in human, physical terms.

Hopefully, the Self will reach a point where it is able to manifest the essence of who and what it is in one physical incarnation. Each of these incarnations expresses a version of the greater Self; each of your lives is a portion of your total experience. Eventually, when the Self has expressed itself as fully as possible within the physical dimension, an incarnation may occur in which, in its earthly persona, the Self knows itself for what it truly is. At this point we become aware of our other incarnations, our other lives; we consciously lay claim to all of our experiences in the physical dimension as they have played out in the context of time.

This view implies that the Self has the capacity or potential to express itself in dimensions of reality other than the physical. Perhaps after we have completed our experiences of this dimension, we will move on to experience ourselves in the context of other reality systems, other dimensions. At present we cannot conceive of what the nature of such existences might be. Nevertheless, we cannot assume that the physical dimension is the only reality in which a Self or gestalt of consciousness may express its nature.

Finally, there is one other possibility that is interesting to think about. What would prevent the Self from manifesting more than one version of itself in our dimension during one time period? Could it be that the greater gestalt of consciousness from which we spring is able to pursue more than one "incarnation" at a time? I see no reason to assume out of hand that we must be the sole version of our greater natures in physical existence at any given time. We may have counterparts or alternate selves living right now, individuals who in the greater context of things are one with us, but who for necessity's sake would be perceived as "separate" individuals. This might explain the propensity of some people to seek a "soul mate."

Each of the above scenarios entails the ability of the Self to express its nature through the guise of more than one self or personality. Truly, it would be naive of us to assume that who and what we are now is the total expression of all that we are in the deepest sense. Each expression of the greater Self, ultimately, is an expression of who and what we are. This is no more far-fetched than saying that the child you were at the age of six was a partial expression of the total self that you are in this life. That child's experiences are part of your experiences, even though you are no longer that child. Likewise, the experiences of an incarnated version of your greater Self in the sixteenth century may be part of your experiences, even though you may think of yourself as being only who you are here and now.

Subjectivity, Objectivity, and the Reach of Mind

The preceding material, though somewhat beyond the scope of an investigation into the objective reality of the mind's energies, is important because of the nature of the experiences one may encounter through any exploration of the mindscape. Not everything you encounter within your mind can be related directly to your current physical life. To understand our minds, we need to understand something of the multidimensional nature of consciousness, since the mind serves not only in our relationships with physical reality, but also as our connection with other aspects of our being.

Many aspects of reality have escaped us because we have clung to limiting notions of the self. It is a traditional conceit in the West to give paramount importance to the experiences of the physical self. It is true that our current experience of reality is concentrated within the physical dimension. But to consider these experiences as the center of existence is like believing the Earth is the center of the solar system. So long as we assume that reality revolves about our experiences of the physical, the greater mysteries of reality will escape us.

In the final part of this book I summarize the mind's relationship with reality as we know it and the implications of such a relationship. But there is one last subject I want to cover in this chapter, a subject involving the issues of subjectivity, objectivity, and the reach of mind.

Throughout this book I have attempted to present evidence in support of the concept of the objective reality of thoughts, emotions, ideas, and the other patterns within the mind. I recognize that this is somewhat misleading. What do we really mean when we say that something is objectively valid?

According to Webster's Dictionary, something is objective when it is "of or having to do with a known or perceived object as distinguished from something existing only in the mind of the subject, or person thinking." The secondary definition lists "objective" as "being, or regarded as being, independent of the mind; real; actual." [1] So the very language that we use predisposes us against considering anything within the mind as real. Therefore, according to standard usage of language, anything that is mental is unreal. The statement that the products of the mind are objective seems a contradiction.

Fortunately, language does not dictate the nature of reality; it merely reflects our current conceptions regarding reality. I hope to demonstrate that the concept of an objective reality independent of the mind involves a totally erroneous approach to reality, and that reality is a totally subjective affair.

In the first place, we can have no experiences even of purely physical reality independently of the mind. We say that we see an object "out there" and separate from us. But we cannot see that object without the physical sense of vision, and we cannot interpret the visual signals without the brain. Furthermore, nothing in the brain makes any sense without the operations of mind. So all of our experiences of physical reality are coordinated within the mind. Therefore, we cannot say that we perceive objective, physical reality, since we cannot relate to or perceive this reality without the mind.

We have also seen through the discoveries of quantum physicists that the observer of an event affects the manifestation of that event. The very atoms that compose our physical reality react to the influences of our minds. Once again, objectivity is destroyed. This suggests that our attitude and stance in relation to any event affects the nature of that event.

The evidence is overwhelmingly in support of the contention that our moods, attitudes, and psychological frames of mind color our perceptions of the world. We react more to what we believe to be real than to what is "objectively real." Is there any way to disassociate ourselves from our own psychological states in order to perceive objective reality? Can we get beyond our minds in order to witness this elusive objective world?

The core of our being is our consciousness. It exists prior to all perceptions and relationships. It is the starting point of all that we know or perceive. We may never fully fathom its ultimate nature because we can never look at our own consciousness directly. It is like the eye trying to see itself.

What does our consciousness see then, but the expression of its own nature and the nature of other gestalts of consciousness, as they are mirrored in reality. The first expressions of consciousness, then, are the constituent energies of mind. The nature of this "first" mind is beyond our current recognition. It is associated with that vast gestalt that divides itself into component selves. It relates to and perceives all the dimensions to which it has access.

The mind with which we as individuals are familiar is but a part of this vast mind. Ordinary functions of the mind relate to the reality of the self with which we primarily identify. But vaster aspects of mind still hover about, so that we are connected to the central gestalt of consciousness. The mind that we know is an expression of our total consciousness.

This individual mind formulates or conceives ideas and mental patterns, and these give rise to emotions and other energies. These ideas and their attendant energies are selectively sorted and then propelled into physical manifestation. Out of the various dimensions of mind rise those events that we experience in physical reality. Therefore, the events we experience are expressions of the mind, which is in turn an expression of our total consciousness.

So where does mind end and objective reality begin? It seems that the question is not about the objective nature of thoughts and mental energies. It seems that it is about the subjective nature of all the reality that we experience. Objectivity is a concept based upon the outmoded view of reality as composed of distinct and separate parts. Once this view is overthrown, as in the new physics, then everything becomes subjective.

So, are thoughts and emotions objectively real? No. But neither is physical reality objectively real. The mind and its energies and the physical world both have the same kind of reality.

Finally, it may seem that in this picture, with its positioning of the individual self, that you and I are fairly insignificant in the scheme of things. But I do not believe this is the case. That which we call God must be the first consciousness, the consciousness that encompasses all that is. It would be reasonable to assume that this first consciousness divides into an infinite number of vast gestalts that further divide again and again as the process of Self-expression progresses. Somewhere along the line, the consciousness from which arise all of our probable selves enters the picture. Out of that we arise.

Is our greater consciousness made insignificant because it is seemingly dwarfed by greater gestalts of consciousness, which are seemingly dwarfed by God? Is the self with which we identify made insignificant because there is something that perceives a wider expanse of reality?

Every aspect of consciousness is an expression of the infinite One Consciousness. Every aspect is part of the whole and contributes to the experience of the whole. In the final analysis there is only one of us, but that One can express itself in infinite natures.

Each self, while being part of a greater whole, is relatively autonomous. Free will exists everywhere, and the choices and actions of each contribute to the expression and experience of all. No part is insignificant; no self is insignificant.

The myriad aspects of the All may choose to form new groupings. We may, at any time, open ourselves to become more aware of our greater natures. We may evolve into that which we seem to be but a part of now. In a linear time perspective our greater Self is our future self. Beyond the parameters of our private selves we already are our greater Selves; we have simply forgotten it, at least for the duration of our current physical life-span.

So, what are the boundaries of mind? None. What are the boundaries of selfhood? None. And what are the boundaries of consciousness? There are none.

The infinity of reality is open to us through exploring our mindscape. But we are physically incarnated for a purpose. There is something important to learn here. It has to do with the powers of creation, some of which are at our disposal. So let's return to Earth and matters at hand.

Epilogue

There is far more to our existence than simple survival and observing the experiences physical life has to offer. We are consciousness in the process of evolution. Learning to live and function effectively within the physical domain is critical to this process, but learning these things requires that we look at more than just the physical.

That which we perceive around us is the manifestation of our own inner natures. As written in *The Tibetan Book of the Great Liberation,* "All appearances are verily one's own concepts, self-conceived in the mind, like reflections seen in a mirror." [1] What we see is an extension of who and what we are. We are cocreators, and that which we create is an expression of the level of understanding at which we have arrived.

This physical system of reality, this world which we so often consider to be the center of the universe, is a training ground, a classroom. We are learning to be *conscious* cocreators, and the physical dimension is our laboratory. Even on a purely physical level, this learning process is self-evident, or at least it should be so. Everything we do offers evidence of our task and responsibility. Our environment reflects the way we use nature's resources; correct action results in nature's bounty and our own healthy sustenance; incorrect action results in pollution and dangers to our health and that of other creatures. The relationships we create with others determine the social environment in which we live. Our understanding and right application of the laws of physical nature give us the power to create civilizations, to erect mighty structures, and to harness nature's powers. Is there any question but that on the physical level we fashion our own world?

Once we have learned that we are responsible for our physical actions, we must come to understand the source of our physical actions. As Emerson said: "We know that the ancestor of every action is a thought." [2] This is not simply figurative; it is a literal truth. The world of things is born from the seeds of mind. Our reality springs forth according to the dictates of mind, and according to the greater purposes of the total Self.

The lesson remains the same—to understand how and to what degree we participate in the creation of our own reality, and to take responsibility for our share of the creation process. The difference lies in the realm in which we work. On mastering the physical we must begin to master the mental. As the philosopher Blaise Pascal said: "All our dignity consists, then, in thought. By it we must elevate ourselves, and not by space and time which we cannot fill. Let us endeavor, then, to think well; this is the principle of morality." [3]

It may be helpful to summarize briefly some of the material covered thus far:

1. Our thoughts, emotions, beliefs, and other mental patterns and structures are composed of subtle energies which reside within the mental dimen-

sion and which go out to influence the minds of others and physical reality.

2. Our mental energy fields attract similar mental energies and repel dissimilar ones.

3. These fields group together to form the web-work of the personal mental matrix, through which we perceive reality and according to which we participate in the shaping of reality.

4. Our physical experiences coalesce about the mental energies of the self, in line with the designs of the greater Self, yielding our experience of life.

5. As evidenced on the subatomic level, nonphysical energies and probable events are selected and propelled into physical materialization.

What, then, are the practical applications of such knowledge? First, it implies that we are in control of our own mental states. We determine the nature of the thoughts, emotions, and beliefs within our own minds. By applying this knowledge we can effectively increase our powers of understanding, and we can establish our own psychological well-being. We can eliminate undesired mental patterns and encourage and increase desired mental energies. In other words, we have the power and responsibility to determine the contents of our own minds, thereby freeing ourselves for greater inner harmony and for greater discoveries regarding the nature of reality and our own nature.

Second, we can, to a significant degree, consciously determine the nature of our experiences in physical reality. Our desired life-scenario unfolds as we master the mind's processes. We can draw experiences to ourselves according to our consciously chosen intentions and purposes. We can create a totally fulfilling life by applying knowledge of the mind's true nature. We create our private experience of reality consciously or unconsciously, but through conscious recognition of the importance of our beliefs and mental energies, and through a disciplined application of this knowledge, we can create the experience of reality that we choose. We can be aware that we are doing this.

Finally, since we collectively shape our public reality, we may with full awareness influence the way humanity's history progresses. A clear, concise, and strong mental thought of peace has more power than a hundred unfocused, uncertain thoughts of war. We have the power to create a truly golden age for humanity, and that power lies within our minds.

The practical applications of the realization that your thoughts are real and serve to shape your experience of reality are truly endless. Nothing thwarts the realization of your desires but your own mind. Nothing limits your abilities for greater realization but your own beliefs. Recognition of the reality of mental energies brings immense power and great freedom. However, increased responsibility comes in the wake of increased freedom and power.

Whether or not you recognize and acknowledge the effects of your mental actions, you are responsible for them. You are just as responsible for a violent thought as you are for a violent physical action. No matter how private your thoughts may seem, their influence goes beyond your own mental space. There is no punishment implied in wrong thinking; there is only the result of reaping the effects of your own creations. Our experiences of reality mirror our inner states, so that we may see clearly what we are doing and make necessary changes.

It is not complicated to apply morality and ethics to the domain of mind. We have had centuries to learn how we should treat one another. We know what is right and wrong. We have only to apply familiar ethical and moral tenets to our thoughts, beliefs, and emotions. Take any of the moral precepts or religious laws by which you think life should be governed and apply them to your mind. You will have a guideline for mental morality. Thou shalt not kill; thou shalt not think of killing. Or consider Kant's categorical imperative: govern your behavior according to those principles that you would have govern the behavior of all people. Likewise, think according to those principles that you would have govern the thoughts of all people. Just as you should not perpetrate physical violence upon another, so should you not perpetrate mental or psychic violence. I offer a new rule: think of others as you would have them think of you.

We are destined to continue our existence beyond our physical lives, into nonphysical dimensions. In such dimensions there will be far fewer buffers between our mental states and our experiences of reality. I believe that we will not be allowed to exercise our powers fully in such realms until we have learned to take responsibility for our mental states and mental actions. Our existence in physical reality affords us the opportunity to learn this lesson and to master our minds. We reap what we sow, and until we understand that we sow with our minds, we will be kept in the classroom of physical reality.

Our responsibilities are great because our powers are great. We truly were created in the image of God, because we were given the power of creation. First we learn to accept our physical responsibilities; then we learn to accept our mental responsibilities. Only then will we be free to fly into the infinite reaches of reality.

Notes

PREFACE

1. Charles W. Leadbeater, *The Inner Life* (Wheaton, IL: Theosophical Publishing House, 1978), p. 284.
2. Christmas Humphreys, *Buddhism* (Baltimore, MD: Penguin Books, 1951), pp. 152-153.
3. Ralph Waldo Emerson, "Nature," *Emerson's Essays* (New York, NY: Thomas Y. Crowell Co., 1926), p. 400.
4. C. G. Jung, *On The Nature Of The Psyche,* translated by R. F. C. Hull (Princeton, NJ: Princeton University Press, 1960), p. 7.
5. Ibid., p. 66.

CHAPTER 1

1. René Descartes, "Discourse on the Method of Rightly Conducting the Reason and Seeking for Truth in the Sciences," *Descartes: Selections* (New York, NY: Charles Scribner's Sons, 1955), p. 7.
2. J. B. Rhine, *New Frontiers of the Mind: The Story of the Duke Experiments* (Westport, CT: Greenwood Press, 1972), pp. 268-269.
3. Louisa E. Rhine, *Mind Over Matter: Psychokinesis* (London: Macmillan, 1970), p. 356.
4. Bruce A. Vance, *Dreamscape: Voyage in an Alternate Reality* (Wheaton, IL: Theosophical Publishing House, 1989).

5. Joseph Chilton Pearce, *Exploring the Crack in the Cosmic Egg* (New York, NY: Julian Press, 1974), pp. 153-155.

6. Charles A. Leadbeater, *The Inner Life* (Wheaton, IL: Theosophical Publishing House, 1978) p. 294.

7. Ibid., pp. 294-296.

8. Ibid., p. 291.

Chapter 2

1. Annie Besant, *Man and His Bodies* (Wheaton, IL: Theosophical Publishing House), 1967.

2. Nick Herbert, *Quantum Reality: Beyond the New Physics* (Garden City, NY: Anchor Press / Doubleday, 1985).

3. Michael Talbot, *Beyond the Quantum* (New York, NY: Bantam Books, 1988), p. 181.

4. Carl Jung, *Four Archetypes* (Princeton, NJ: Princeton University Press, 1973), pp. 3-4.

5. Charles W. Leadbeater, *The Inner Life* (Wheaton, IL: Theosophical Publishing House, 1978), p. 292.

6. Charles T. Tart, *States of Consciousness* (New York: E. P. Dutton, 1975), pp. 30-31.

7. Carl Jung, *Four Archetypes.*

8. Bruce A. Vance, *Dreamscape.*

9. Robert Monroe, *Far Journeys* (New York, NY: Doubleday, 1985), p. 3.

Chapter 3

1. W. Y. Evans-Wentz, ed., *The Tibetan Book of the Great Liberation* (London: Oxford University Press, 1954), p. 236.

2. Ram Dass, *Journey of Awakening: A Meditator's Guidebook* (New York, NY: Bantam Books, 1981), pp. 26-27.

3. Bruce A. Vance, *Dreamscape.*

4. Murray Wright Bundy, *The Theory of Imagination in*

Classical and Mediaeval Thought (Urbana, IL: University of Illinois Press, 1928), pp. 57-58.

5. Charles T. Tart, ed., *Altered States of Consciousness* (Garden City, NY: Doubleday, 1969), pp. 1-2.
6. Bruce A. Vance, *Dreamscape.*
7. Stephen LaBerge, *Lucid Dreaming* (New York, NY: Ballantine Books, 1985).
8. Patricia Garfield, *Creative Dreaming* (New York, NY: Ballantine Books, 1974).
9. Bruce A. Vance, *Dreamscape.*
10. Janet Lee Mitchell, *Out-of-Body Experiences: A Handbook* (New York, NY: Ballantine Books, 1981).
11. Robert Monroe, *Journeys Out of the Body* (Garden City, NY: Doubleday, 1971).
12. Robert Monroe, *Far Journeys* (New York, NY: Doubleday, 1985).
13. Ibid., p. 3.
14. Mircea Eliade, *Shamanism: Archaic Technique of Ecstasy* (Princeton, NJ: Princeton University Press, 1972).
15. Michael Harner, *The Way of the Shaman* (New York, NY: Bantam Books, 1982).

CHAPTER 4

1. Beatrice Bruteau, *The Psychic Grid: How We Create the World We Know* (Wheaton, IL: Theosophical Publishing House, 1979), p. 154.
2. *The Gospel According to Luke,* 11:9.

CHAPTER 5

1. Ralph Waldo Emerson, "History," *Emerson's Essays* (New York, NY: Thomas Y. Crowell, 1926), p. 1.

CHAPTER 6

1. Charles T. Tart, *States of Consciousness* (New York, NY: E. P. Dutton, 1975), p. 253.

CHAPTER 7

1. Annie Besant, *A Study In Consciousness* (Madras, India: Theosophical Publishing House, 1980), p. 119.
2. Ibid., p. 105.

CHAPTER 8

1. Michael Talbot, *Beyond the Quantum* (New York, NY: Bantam Books, Inc., 1987), pp. 19-21.
2. Ibid., p. 38.
3. Ibid., p. 150.
4. Ibid., p. 151.
5. Fred Alan Wolf, *Parallel Universes: The Search for Other Worlds* (New York, NY: Simon & Schuster, 1988), p. 143.
6. Ibid., p. 204.
7. David Bohm, *Wholeness and the Implicate Order* (London: Routledge & Kegan Paul, 1981), p. 72.
8. Ibid., pp. 124-125.
9. Ibid., p. 134.
10. Ibid.
11. Karl Pribram, *Consciousness and the Brain* (New York, NY: Plenum, 1976).
12. Talbot, *Beyond the Quantum*, pp. 51-52.
13. Rupert Sheldrake, *A New Science of Life: The Hypothesis of Formative Causation* (London: Blond & Briggs, 1981).

CHAPTER 9

1. *Webster's New World Dictionary* (Cleveland, and New York: World Publishing Co., 1966), p. 1012.

EPILOGUE

1. W. Y. Evans-Wentz, ed., *The Tibetan Book of the Great Liberation* (London: Oxford University Press, 1954), p. 215.

2. Ralph Waldo Emerson, "Spiritual Laws," *Emerson's Essays*, p. 117.
3. Blaise Pascal, "Thoughts," *The European Philosophers from Descartes to Nietzsche*, Monroe C. Beardsley, ed., (New York, NY: Random House, 1960), p. 128.

Quest
Books

We publish books on:

Healing and Health ● Occultism and
Mysticism ● Transpersonal Psychology
Philosophy ● Religion ● Reincarnation,
Theosophical Philosophy ● Yoga and Meditation.

Other books of possible interest include:

Beyond the Post-Modern Mind *by Huston Smith*
Revised edition reviews latest ideas in science and theology.

East Meets West *edited by Rosemarie Stewart*
Our higher nature and transpersonal psychological
implications.

From Atom to Kosmos *by L. Gordon Plummer*
Astronomy's stupendous universe theory relates to
mysticism.

Fullness of Human Experience *by Dane Rudhyar*
How cyclic nature of creation affects our psychic evolution.

Inner Adventures *by E. Lester Smith*
Eminent scientist probes limits of thought and intuition.

Rhythm of Wholeness *by Dane Rudhyar*
We are part and parcel of the wholeness that always is.

The Theatre of the Mind *by Henryk Skolimowski*
The scope and importance of our evolution.

Two Faces of Time *by Lawrence W. Fagg*
Comparative study of time as viewed by religion and
science.

The Wholeness Principle *by Anna Lemkow*
U. N. economist shows how all life is interdependent and
unitive.

Available from:
The Theosophical Publishing House
P. O. Box 270, Wheaton, Illinois 60189-0270